POT BELLY PIGS

Pot Belly Pigs Complete Owner's Guide.

Pot Bellied Pigs care, health, temperament, training, senses, costs, feeding and activities.

by

Roger Radford

Table of Contents

Foreword

Owning a pet can be really exciting, especially when you become a pet owner for the first time. This is also a very difficult job, as new pet owners do not know what is best for their pets.

It may sound weird to others that you have a pet pig, but aren't they adorable? Pigs are unique and are divided into many breeds, from which come the pot belly pigs. Taking care of pigs is a whole other ballgame, as compared to other animals.

From different colors right down to their cuteness, not to forget their mischief, learn everything you need to know about your pet from this professional guide. From breeds to food all the way to license and insurance, you will find all of your answers right here.

Make sure you go through this guide word for word before you purchase your little piggy. In order to help you along, Piggie and her friends will be at your assistance.

Happy reading!

Introduction

Pigs are very intelligent animals, especially potbellied pigs. These exotic animals are not common when it comes to owning pets, but how can you look away from their adorable eyes and that cute pink nose? Owning a pet is a big decision no matter how easy it may seem.

These little guys may look small which is why many doubt that owning one will not be easy, but that is not always true. Owning a pet means you are taking full responsibility.

Potbellied pigs are usually smaller in size comparatively to other average farm pigs that are found in America as well as in the UK. They have been given their name because of the shape of their bellies. They are also considered as the same species as wild boars and farm pigs.

Potbellied pigs have the capability to breed with other species of pigs as well. They may be brought up in different locations. These little pigs are very friendly and can socialize really well no matter where they are brought up.

Chapter 1: The History of the Pot Bellied Pig

The pot bellied pigs have a very interesting and long history. Originating from Asia, these pigs are known popularly to be from their Vietnamese background. Families used the pot bellied pigs as a source of food and fat. Unlike the other farm pigs who have a fat proportion of 5-20%, pot bellied pigs are 50% fat.

In the past 100 years the pigs came to Europe. Their breed started to become very popular. Then during the midst of the 80s a man named Connell shipped them off to Canada. There they were used to conduct many experiments due to their efficient size, and they are relatively close to the regular farm pigs and hogs.

During the late 80s, Connell pigs were then shifted off to America, where they were displayed in zoos. The zoo owners had them bred and sold their offspring and the breed gained popularity rapidly.

The pigs were often sold to farmers and breeders during this time. The farmers and breeders eventually bred the pigs with other bloodlines, creating mixed breeds. These mixed breeds were selected and put through competitions to see which one had created the best one.

The winners of the competition were then sold for a lot of money. During this pink era, the first pot bellied pig association came forth. The pigs were registered, were researched on, and their entire history had been chased all the way back to Vietnam. In fact, some very surprising information which came forth was that pot bellied pigs are descendants of the Chinese pigs who were domesticated 10,000 years ago!

Unfortunately, these pigs were abandoned after they lost their popular standing. The association also stopped registering the pigs, and they were left all alone. With no proper care, food source, and required treatment, the pot bellied pigs faced severe malnutrition problems.

Thus came along the teacups; these are actually the malnutrition breed of the pot bellied pigs due to their size and weight, although their organs are completely normal.

As time passed, many people adopted these pigs as farm animals, either for a source of food and fat, to breed for offspring, or to keep them as pets. The pot bellied pigs became popular as pets, especially the teacups due to their size. They were the same size as farm pigs, and were fun to keep, as they easily got along.

As the years continued, more breeders mixed the bloodline of the potbellied pigs with others. Most of them bred the pot bellied pigs with farm hogs as they are known to be cousins and are quite similar to each other.

Nowadays, all of the pot bellied pigs in the United States are known to be mix breeds and not genuine pot bellied. The several breeds which were created include the Swedish White, Juliana, KuneKune, Teacup, and the Guinea Hogs.

Chapter 2: Piggie's Different Breeds

Piggie belongs to the family of wild boars and farm pigs. Potbellied pigs are known as mini pigs because of their size. Mini pigs also include KuneKune pigs, Teacups, and Guinea Hogs. They all are cousins so to speak and look remarkably alike.

Brief Comparisons of the Breeds

The potbellied pigs weigh in at a massive 43 to 136 kg. The KuneKune pig, on the other hand weighs around 400 pounds, which is close enough to the weight of an average farm pig. The Guinea hog is different in terms of looks. Unlike the potbellied pigs and KuneKune, the hogs are a bit thinner and taller, and can be compared to a large pot in terms of size.

The Teacups or also known as Micro Minis are also potbellied pigs. Unfortunately due to malnutrition and other health concerns, their size and weight is not up to the average potbellied pig. However, even though these pigs remain tiny, the size of their organs remains normal.

KuneKune Pigs

The KuneKune pigs are actually a line of pot bellied pigs which have been bred with each other containing different or the same bloodlines. These pigs have been around since the 1900s and were known for their popularity in New Zealand. The name KuneKune means 'round and fat,' just like the pigs.

In the midst of the 20th century these pigs became a popular source of pork. Near the 1980s, they almost became extinct; in fact hardly 50 KuneKune pigs were left. This is when farmers resorted to mixed breeding and the KuneKune pigs became a part of a recovery program, which began in New Zealand to save the breed, which was quite successful.

KuneKune Appearance
The KuneKune are really easy to spot. This breed of pot belly pigs are hairy, come in different colors, and are covered in spots. Their hair color even varies with pink, ginger, cream, gold, white, tan, and black. Another way in which you can easily identify them is by their lower jaw. The KuneKunes have tassel jaws, which mean their lower jaw has piri piri under its chin. The pigs are short, round, as their name says, and have small legs. Their average height is of 60 cm.

Vietnamese Potbellied pig
Many of these pigs have been abandoned by their owners because their pig was growing a lot larger than what they expected. Because the body of a Vietnamese pot belly pig is very solid and compact, these pigs can weigh up to 200 pounds without being overweight. The average weight is between 120 and 140 pounds.

Teacups
The teacup pigs are the offspring of four of the main pig breeds, one of which is the pot bellied pigs. The mix bloodline of the pot

belly and other breeds such as KuneKune result in the teacup. Due to the play of genetics, the pigs are small, which is why they are also known as micro pigs, mini pot bellies, etc.

Fake breeders or owners who lack information on the teacups will assure you that they remain of the same size throughout their lifespan, which is not true. Teacups can grow, and they do not remain the same size all their lives. If a breeder or an owner tells you this, there are two reasons behind it, either they have starved the pigs, or they are themselves unaware regarding the breed.

Teacup Appearance
The teacup pigs are really adorable. They are small in size but can eventually grow up to be 15 inches; some even grow to be larger than that as well. The teacups weigh less than 55 pounds, but their weight can exceed this as well. Commonly kept as pets, there is no breed which has been properly established under their name. The pigs vary in color depending on the parents or the owners, can have spots, are small in size, and are fun to play with.

Chapter 3: 101 on Taking Piggie and Her Friends Home

When it comes to potbellied pigs, you must gather all the information you need to ensure you can give it the best care possible. Some pet owners take guardianship over the pigs when they are born from breeders, whereas others prefer taking them from a friend.

Taking Guardianship from a Breeder or Owner

When you decide to take guardianship of a potbellied pig, you must make sure you have all the information regarding it. This information includes the pig's diet, health care, habits, etc. These questions are very important as the breeder already has an idea of how to take care of the pig, whereas you, as a new pet owner, do not.

Remember to ask the following questions from the breeder.

How long have you been breeding potbellied pigs for?

It is important to gain information on the breeder as well. You do not want to risk the health of your pet on the information provided by someone who is new. You should ask a professional breeder who has been breeding for quite a few years now.

What makes potbellied pigs unique according to you?

Asking such questions will let you know if the breeder actually knows about his pigs. It is important for the breeder to take interest in the species they breed, as without the proper care and concern, the animal will face problems in development.

Who are the parents? How many litters do they give?

It is very important for you to know who the parents are. Inspect the parents yourself to ensure they are healthy pigs and did not suffer from malnutrition or other health issues. It is also very important to know how many litters the parents are producing as giving birth to too many can result in health issues for the parents, and can cause abnormalities in the baby.

Can breeding many babies cause any abnormality or genetic diseases?

This is a very important question. Usually it is hard to detect if the baby pig has been affected with any genetic disease until symptoms crop up. Abnormality is also hard to detect as signs and symptoms do not appear immediately.

Do you have any medical records of the baby and the parents?

Vaccinations are important no matter which animal you decide to own. Your pet's health should be your first priority which is why you must ask the breeder to provide authentic medical reports as well as vaccine certificates.

Is the piglet ready to be separated?

Often, when a baby is removed or taken away from its parents, it does not react in a positive way. This is why it is necessary for you to ask the breeder if the piglet has been far away from the parents. Many pets due to the same reason do not eat or drink which causes concerns for the owner as well.

Does the piglet get along with other piglets?

Socializing for pet pigs is also very important. Just like how we need friends, they also need someone who can become their play friend and companion.

Can the piglet socialize with other pets?

This can be the tricky part. Potbellied pigs are not able to socialize with other pets such as dogs. Many pet owners already own a dog which makes things a tad more difficult. Dogs are natural hunters and pigs are natural prey, which is why they make a lethal combination.

What is their appropriate diet?

Pet owners feed their pets almost anything and everything, because they love them so much. However, this backfires most of the time. Some pets cannot handle human food as their stomach has a different way of operating. This is especially true for pot bellied pigs.

What hassles should I be prepared for?

Taking care of piglets is a lot of work, and it sure can get messy. Pigs are natural magnets to trouble and messes. They love to chill out in the mud, play and get down and dirty. Baby piglets are mischievous which is why they can be hard to handle at times. A genuine breeder will be able to give you all the information and documents you need. The breeder will also be able to give you extra tips, which you can use to take care of your potbellied piglet. Ask experienced owners for more authentic and up to date information regarding their care. The breeder will also ask you questions to see if you can take care of the pigs. Be prepared to answer them because if you are not knowledgeable enough, the breeder may not hand over the piglet or the piglets.

The following are some questions that a typical breeder may ask and how you can tackle them:

Do you have any experience with potbellied pigs?

Be honest to the breeder, even if you have no experience with pigs at all. Lying will not get you anywhere and it will not be healthy for the piglet either. If you are not experienced, the breeder will give you tips on how you can take better care of your pet.

Have you had any experience with other pets?

If you are a newbie pet owner be honest with the breeder; they will help you have a better understanding of how you can bond with your pet and how you can take care of it.

Do you know about their diet?

Each animal has a unique diet; they cannot have regular food like humans as their bodies function differently.

Are you updated with the kind of health care they require?

Pets require love and care, but they also require proper checkups and health care as well. This includes vaccinations. It is important for you to understand the importance of every vaccination shot.

Do you have enough space to own a pig?

Pigs, love wide and open spaces. These pets are best and properly taken care of if they are residing in the backyard or in the front yard of the house. The yards will allow them to roam around and play more than the average space they will get within the residence.

Will you be able to handle more than one pet?

It can be difficult to handle more than one pet at the same time. Potbellied pigs love to socialize so you should have no issue there, but you will still face difficulty managing them.

This includes cleaning up after them, managing your household with these pets as they are playful and sometimes they can get out of hand as well and ensuring you allot enough money each month for their healthcare and food. Plus as they grow older and bigger, the costs of medication and their food will also rise.

Which other pets do you have?

Pigs get along fine with other pigs, but not so well with other animals that are predators such as dogs. If you have one, emphasize how you will ensure it does not hurt your pigs.

Where do you live?

Pet pigs need an open environment in order to grow naturally. This means that if you reside in an apartment, flat, condo, or any such residence which does not have a yard or extra space outdoors for a pet, you will not be able to accommodate it.

Why do you want to adopt a pig?

Do you really want to adopt the potbellied pig because of their heart touching cuteness? The breeder or farmer will want to know your intentions behind this adoption to see if you have really thought your decision through.

Are you aware of the law?

Countries and states have different laws based on pets. These are important as they protect the rights of the animal. If any of the rules and regulations are violated, the pet will be taken away from its current owner.

Chapter 4: 1 Piggy, 2 Piggies, 3 Piggies or 4?

One confusion all pet owners have regarding any pet is how many should they own. You will also think to yourself, should I only get one? Won't he or she get lonely? Should I get more?

One pig can get very lonely without a companion. Two pigs are plenty as well. However, do keep in mind that these little piglets will not remain little all their lives. They can grow incredibly fast and can eat a lot.

Positives of Owning One Pig
Taking responsibility of a single pig is much easier for new owners. You can save more money on food, vaccines and especially veterinarian bills, cleaning up after the piglet will be easier as well and by giving undivided attention to one swine you will ensure it enjoys a long and happy life.

Negatives of Owning One Pig
Eventually, after being separated from its parents and siblings, the piglet will get lonely. It may change its eating habits due to the same reason, which can cause health concerns.

Positives of Owning more than One Pig
Getting another piglet as a companion will ensure the abovementioned issues do not crop up. More than one piglet

means your little piglet will not be lonely anymore. The piglet will eat properly and not face any health issues and will remain happy. The piglet will also learn how to interact with other pets as well.

Negatives of Owning more than One Pig

More than one piglet means more responsibilities. This also means the food will increase, more space will eventually be occupied, more vaccines to be kept up with, and more messes to clean up after.

Laws and Regulations of Owning Pigs

The place where you reside will have laws on owning pigs. If you reside within the United States, keep in mind that each law is different for each state. The same will be the case if you live in the UK.

Laws and Regulations for the United States

You must first confirm with City Hall if you are eligible to adopt a potbellied pig. Mainly, it is illegal to own a potbellied pig in the United States. Even though they are considered illegal, incorporated cities allow it.

Even if the individual behind the desk says they are illegal, ask them to give you a copy of the state law which states that these pigs cannot be held or adopted as pets. Many times individuals assume that they are illegal when there is still a chance for you to adopt the pigs.

If you can adopt a pet potbellied pig legally, still ask them for a copy of the state law which states so.

When you adopt a pig, make sure it does not bother your neighbors. This also includes property damage and diseases it might carry. If your neighbor reports you, you will be held fully responsible in the eyes of the law.

There are also laws in ordinance of the size, weight, number, and zoning of the potbellied pigs as well. Make sure the pig you decide to adopt meets with all requirements as it can cause you trouble later on if it does not meet them.

The average weight of a male potbellied pig should be no more than 100 pounds. This is based upon the orders of the North American Potbellied Pig Association also known as NAPPA. Their rules state that if a male potbellied pig is adopted and is being taken care of as a pet; its weight should not exceed 100 pounds. What NAPPA did not clearly mention was that this applies to potbellied pigs that are 1 year old or less.

Potbellied pigs can be 200 pounds and still not be considered over-weight. Their weight varies between 100-150 pounds at most. A fully grown potbellied pig is of 5 years of age.

If you get permission to keep a potbellied pig under the aegis of the law, remember that the USDA does not consider the potbellied pigs as livestock. According to them, they are pets only. So be sure to check in on the laws first.

Laws and Regulations for United Kingdom
In order to be granted permission of owning a pet in the United Kingdom, you need to apply for a CPH number 15 days prior to purchasing your pet potbellied pig. In the United Kingdom, pigs are considered as livestock, not pets, but you will still require a CPH number in order for this allowance. This rule is different for different locations in England, Scotland and Wales.

CPH Number
A CPH number stands for Country Parish Holding. This number is given to pet pigs and is issued by DEFRA so that no one can take away the pig from the owner. The number gives the potbellied pig the identity of being a pet.

How to Obtain a CPH Number

Getting a CPH number is not very hard at all. You must call the Rural Payments Agency's Customer Service Center in order to apply for it. They will request some basic information such as your name, address, and a few more details such as where you will be keeping the livestock.

Chapter 5: Piggie & Friends

Potbellied pigs like Piggie and her friends cannot get enough of socializing. Potbellied pigs easily befriend each other as well as other pigs. Before you decide to take a potbellied pig home, you must consider the following:

- The Potbellied Pig must be older than 8 weeks.
- If you own other pets you must visit a pet behavior specialist.
- Make sure you have enough space for the Potbellied Pig(s).
- Make sure your new pets have been vaccinated before you bring them home.
- Let the Potbellied Pig(s) roam around and explore their new habitat. They will take time to adapt to the other pets, the surroundings and you as well.
- Potbellied Pigs are trainable, but training them is very complex.
- Keep dangerous objects out of the way of the piglet(s). It is highly important to watch out for literally everything the piglet(s) does.
- The pigs will adapt to other animals easily but it will take hard work and time.

Children & Potbellied Pigs

Children do not always expect to have potbellied pigs as pets, and often they do not get along. Some children love pigs, take care of them, and treat them like any other pet. Those children are more likely to get along with a pet potbellied pig.

Potbellied pigs are very intelligent pets. They can easily sense if their owners care for them or not. This ability helps them socialize more with children who prefer pigs as pets.

Potbellied Pigs & Cats

Pigs and cats get along well, mostly. However, this will depend on the nature of the two you own. If your cat is jealous of other animals, it will likely feel the same way towards your pet pig. Similarly, your pig may have difficulty socializing with your pet cat.

Potbellied Pigs & Dogs

Dogs are natural predators, which makes this an issue. Dogs and pigs do not get along. This can be made possible but via a lengthy and a very complex process. You will have to take your pet dog to a behavior specialist who will work their relationship out. Even if that does happen, do not leave the two alone in the same room or else the dog will turn into the big bad wolf!

Chapter 6: Health Care

Pigs are no ordinary pets, which means that their care is different compared to those of regular pets such as dogs and cats. You must first understand what the health needs of a pet pot bellied pig are before you bring it home. This includes its feeding habit, habitat, vaccines and much more.

Feeding and Companionship

The first step in feeding your pet pig is to know what pigs eat. Pot bellied pigs have enormous appetites, which basically means they will eat anything you offer them. Unfortunately, many owners do exactly that and feed their pigs what they are not supposed to. This causes health issues with the pig, as its stomach cannot support all the food you feed it.

Since they cannot open the fridge themselves it is important for you as the responsible owner to give your pet a scheduled, balanced diet. Developing a routine creates healthy food habits, which results in a healthy pig, meaning a longer life span.

A pot bellied pig needs a good meal which is high in fibers and low in calories. Some food stores carry diet food especially made for pot bellied and mini pigs. If they are not available in food stores, you can always visit a nearby pet store or order the food online. If that is not an option either, ask your pet's vet to order it for you.

Feeding your Pet Pig Commercial Food

It is not always a good idea to feed your pet pig human food, especially junk. Your pig will love to eat anything you offer but it is unaware of what is healthy for it and what is not. If you do decide to feed your pet commercial food, make sure you avoid foods which are rich for your pigs, too rich that is.

Non breeding pigs which weigh around 25 pounds get ½ cup of food for maintenance. This means if your pet weights 100 pounds, it will get 2 cups of maintenance food. This meal is equivalent to the entire day. In short you will feed your pig one cup twice a day. However, this is dependent on your pig as well, and its body type. If the pig is obese, this diet plan will not suit it. It is best if you ask your vet what plan should you be following then.

If your pet pig is of roughly 6 weeks old, you may feed it according to the routine you wish for it to have and then maintain. Let them eat as much as they want as their bodies are growing till they reach 3 months. After 3 months, their food intake will eventually change and slow down to 1 ½ cups to 1 cup, according to their consumption.

You can even feed your pig healthy vegetables such as celery, cucumbers, carrots, peppers, potatoes, and lots more but try to avoid the starch ones like the potatoes.

Fruits are a good idea as well; you can mix it up a bit and serve your pet a fruit salad with apples and grapes. Many owners use fruits as treats while domesticating their pigs as the animals love juicy apples and grapes.

Many pigs like to chew on the grass as well. Make sure your backyard and front yard, and the entire surrounding perimeter is chemical free and fertilizer free too. The high amount of chemicals, sodium, and potassium is not good for your pet.

Keep this diet plan in mind for a healthy pet as a healthy pet makes a happy home.

Diet Summary
- Diet is important, more fiber and less calories.
- Proper pet food is always the best choice for a pet.
- Do not over feed your pet.
- Do not feed other pet food to your pet pig.

- Avoid fatty food especially chocolate and salty food or snacks.
- Provide your pet pig fresh chemical-free water, lots of it.
- Do not feed the pet from the fridge directly, pigs are smart and can open your fridge, or at least will try to.

Nursing Piglet(s) till 6 Weeks of Age
10 days after being born the piglet should be given a meal with a ratio of 17% to 19% containing protein.

6 Weeks- 3 Months
The pigs now require a 16% protein ratio which gradually decreases to 1- 1 ½ cups a day. At this age it should be fed regularly and with large portions in order for its bones, organs, and nervous system, to develop.

3 Months- 5 Months
14% protein ratio and a maximum of 2 cups per day is good enough for your growing pig. Do not over feed the pig; if the pig's backbone, its ribs, or hip bones are visible to your eyes, you are not feeding the pet enough and it is starving.

5 Months & Older
Give the pig a 14% protein ratio. 12% is also enough and is quite satisfactory. 2 cups per day is enough for your pig to receive all of the needed elements.

Water Needs
Your pet pig will need a lot of fresh water while it is your pet. The best way to provide your pet pig with a fresh source of water is by placing a pot with a wide mouth from which the pig can easily drink from. Make sure the pot is small but wide, so that the pig can drink and not fall into the pot. Micro pigs, piglets, and weaners often fall inside and drown, so it should not exceed a couple of inches.

Another method of providing your pig with water is by having an automatic source. This will require a bit of work from you if you want to set it up yourself or you can call a plumber. In this method, the water will come directly from the water source into an area where the pig can drink from.

If you want to feed your small pot bellied piglets through a feeder, you should go for the metal one. The metal feeder is more durable, long lasting, and due to their sharp teeth and jaw power, it will not break unlike plastic. The feeders can have all internal parts replaced if needed as well.

Water bowls can turn out to be drawbacks. They have to be drained of water, cleaned thoroughly, the water has to be refilled, and then cleaned again especially if it is placed outside in the open air.

Since pigs love to get dirty, play in mud all day long, even for hours, it is common for the water to get dirty as well. You will need a proper wash area, like a shower with water available to clean your pig. Pigs stay cool by rolling in the mud, it may be fun for them, but it will be a headache for you. This is why a proper cleaning area is a good idea.

During the winters, your pet pot belly will need plenty of fresh water as well to keep it from getting dehydrated. Keep in mind that in winters, many states and countries face snowfall as well, so the water source has to be ice free. Select a destination which is proper for all seasons.

Common Diseases
Although having pot bellied pigs as pets is fun and great, there are a few health issues you must first control. Pigs carry diseases, which is why you must first consult with a vet before you bring your pig home. Your pig may be infected with any one of the following diseases, which must be taken care of as soon as possible.

Atrophic Rhinitis

This is an infection which will crop up with a sinus or common cold. It can be caught by other pet pigs if you have more than one in the first couple of days. It is curable and a vet can give you proper medication according to your pet's need.

This disease is transmitted into the young from the mother during feeding from the tit, or from another pig after the young has been weaned off from the mother.

If the disease is very serious, the pig's nose will become distorted as well as its snorts, and this will continue as it grows. This includes a continuous bloody nose and nasal discharges.

Brucellosis

This disease is commonly found in the pot bellied pigs which live in the southern states of Florida, Texas California, and Virginia. The symptoms for this disease include a very severe cold. If a pet pig has such a case, it must be reported to the health ministry, isolated and then later killed. Younger pigs that have this condition lose sensitivity in their spine, experience headaches or facial pain, while older pigs suffer from arthritis, depression or lethargy.

Campylobacteriosis

Campylobacteriosis is a disease which is associated with your pet's stomach. In this, an infection is released into the pig's gastrointestinal system which leads to cramps, vomiting, blood in the stool passage, fever and nausea. This infection can be caught by humans topically through a cut. It is treatable and a vet can help you with this infection.

Porcine Stress Syndrome

It may sound impossible, but pigs can also stress out. PSS in pot bellied pigs is genetic in which the pig loses control of its temper. This can cause sudden death as well. Other symptoms associated with PSS include abnormal breathing, high temperature or abnormal fever, tremors, and joint issues as well. This gene can be made inactive so consult with your vet.

Ringworms

Ringworms are a type of skin infection that is caused by a fungus. If your pet pig has this problem, it will experience hair loss and rashes under the skin in the shape of rings. This is highly contagious but with the right treatment with antibiotics, your vet can bring an end to this problem.

Salmonella

Salmonella is a disease which crops up if the pig comes in contact with the feces of other animals. This disease can be caught by humans as well if your food or water has been exposed to such fecal matter. This is why it is important to keep your pig clean and hygienic. Even after every interaction you have to clean your hands with soap and warm water and do not touch your naked skin while cleaning after your pigs. Remember to clean up after you put on a pair of gloves.

Yersiniosis

This is similar to Salmonella. Although your pot bellied pig will not show any signs and symptoms, it will have bacteria in its intestines, which humans can eventually pick up.

Humans are not immune to the infections and diseases pigs carry, which is why it is important to take up good hygiene practices. Take your pig to the vet often as well for vaccinations.

Bones & Muscle Disorders in Pigs

There are many muscular and bone related disorders your pet pig can also pickup, they include:

Arthritis

This disease can occur in pigs of any age, since the early years as piglets or as fully grown adult pigs. In this disease the joints swell. Sometimes these are visible, but sometimes they are not. It may come about due to arthritis, bacteria, stress, aging, or an inflammation.

If the disease is caused due to bacteria, antibiotics are the best way to fight them off. In other cases the treatment varies depending on the reason behind the cause of the arthritis. Sometimes, a newborn piglet's naval might harbor bacteria that can lead to arthritis. In case it ends up suffering from degenerative arthritis or chronic inflammation that cause joint fusions, the pig may have to be euthanized.

Cracked or Overgrown Hooves
The hooves of your potbellied pig will continue to grow during its entire lifespan. The exotic pigs use their hooves to gain traction on hard and rough surfaces. Since your domestic potbellied pig will not be walking on such hard surfaces like cracked land or concrete, they will need their hooves trimmed.

Untrimmed hooves can cause cracks, which will hurt the pet while walking and the bleeding can lead to infections. If the infection is not taken care of quickly and/or if it gets worse, the hoof and perhaps even the leg may need to be amputated.

Fractures
Fractures can occur due to many reasons as well, rough playing, falling, jumping on furniture, etc. Some fractures may be severe enough to require surgery and even implants such as plates, screws, pins, etc. which can help in the restoration of motion within the body.

In order to prevent such fractures from occurring, the best way is to prevent your pig from being too hyper active, and install a ramp on all stairways.

Lameness
Lameness does not always mean that your pet is lazy. Your pig can go lame if it is injured. This can be clarified through tests, but pigs are not comfortable during them so they will try their best to

give you a hard time. To prevent your pet pot belly from injuring itself further the vet may have to first sedate its hooves, and jaws as well. He/she will then diagnose the reason behind the lameness and prescribe medication for it.

Tetanus
Tetanus is a small infection but can prove to be fatal if left untreated. This is caused by bacteria known as Clostridium Tetani which can be found in your pet pig as well as in humans too. The bacteria enter the body through a wound which is usually caused by rusty metal. It can also manifest if your pig is bitten by another animal.

Symptoms include muscle spasms, muscle contractions, and jaw lock; the inability to open the jaw or mouth. To ensure your pot belly does not succumb to these apply antibiotics on the wound instantly and have a doctor give your pet a tetanus shot.

Brain, Nerve, and Spinal Disorders
Neurological, spinal, and nervous disorders, malfunctions, and failures are often fatal in pets.

Infections
The bacteria that attack the nervous system are mostly escherichia coli, haemophilus parasuis, type 2 streptococcus suis, and salmonella choleraesuis.

They can attack the still developing nervous system of a 6 month old piglet quite easily which is why it needs to be given extra special care as soon as it is born. If the infections are detected an antibiotic course should be started, but be warned the piglet can die even before it shows the signs and symptoms.

Type 2 streptococcus suis can be passed on to humans and vice versa. This is why it is important to take proper care before coming into contact with the pig. Wearing gloves is the best way, and do not touch exposed parts of the body such as your eyes, mouth, or skin to avoid the infection from spreading. Wash your hands with antiseptic soap properly in mild warm water, and make it a daily habit as well.

If you do contract said infection you can experience depression, fever, disorientation, abnormality in posture, coordination issues, seizures and abnormal eye movements.

Poisoning of Salt
If it is cut off from water sources, sudden salt consummation can cause poisoning of salt or toxicity. If the pet has no access to water for at least 36 plus hours this can also cause dehydration. The water exits through the body in the form of drool (saliva) and urine.

This is not common in pet pigs, but it can crop up if they are kept on a salt rich diet. Keeping your domestic pig outside during the cold weather can also be an issue as it is most likely unaware of where to find its source of water.

Signs and symptoms include seizures, blindness, aimless walking, and abnormal posture, sitting, and walking. In such case, a vet should be approached as soon as possible for assistance. Waiting can cause neurological issues such as brain damage, causing further issues in accordance with the treatment.

Seizures
Piglets aged at 1-2 months can have seizures every other day; the duration and occurrence of the seizures can vary. Pigs which do not suffer from too many of these do not need medication. The animals that face regular amounts of seizures are given medication to control them; often, pigs grow out of such episodes as they grow older.

Overheating
The main cause behind your pet overheating is because potbellied pigs do not sweat. When they are exposed to heat and high temperatures, their blood starts to boil and since they cannot sweat, the body has no way to cool off. This can cause your pet to

31

get depressed, inactive, and unresponsive to you as well. If you try to cool your pig with water or mud after it is exposed to heat, the sudden change of temperature can be fatal.

Airway & Lungs Disorders

These disorders make it extremely hard for your pet pig to take in oxygen; this can clog the oxygen supply to their brain, causing brain damage as well. In extreme cases this can lead to death.

Pneumonia

Yes, pigs can catch this disease as well. It is an infection in which the lungs are infected which can lead to signs and symptoms like fever, coughing, and respiratory issues. This infection is common in piglets that can catch it from their mothers or by having contact with other pigs that have been infected. Since pigs already have small lungs, which means the amount of oxygen they regularly intake is already small, an infection like this can easily kill them then.

Antibiotics can be used to treat this disease and some vaccines are also available as well to prevent such an infection from taking place. In some cases, even with urgent treatment, a potbellied pig can lose lung tissue and can then end up suffering from lifelong respiratory problems.

Skin Disorders

Pigs are known to have dry or patchy skin problems; this could be due to the following reasons.

Dry Skin or Flaky Skin

Itching and dry or flaky skin manifests due to many reasons. This can be mild as well as severe in some cases. Do not give your pet pig a bath following this problem as it can make the case worse. Wipe the pig's body with a clean and damp cloth or towel every week to get rid of the flakes. Ask your vet for a moisturizing lotion that you can use to ease its skin condition.

Erysipelas

This disease is caused by an infection created by bacteria known as erysipelothrix rhusiopathiae. In this disease, there are spots visible on the skin. The infection kills skin and tissue cells which can lead to serious issues such as arthritis, and heart problems which can be fatal. If you see patches on your pot bellied pig's then you might need to take it in for treatment. But be careful as this is contagious and can be caught by humans as well.

Sarcoptic Mange

This disease manifests due to mites which reside under the skin. These mites can cause itching and soreness. Infected pigs will try to scratch themselves by either rubbing the affected part against a rough surface or by licking it. A vaccine can be given to the pig to keep mites away as well as to treat an infected pig.

Skin Tumors

Skin tumors are common in swine and potbellied pigs as well. The tumor may even spread to other parts of the body as well depending on the affected part and its condition. The vet can remove the tumor after performing surgery after a pathologist has evaluated the pet. Signs and symptoms include hair loss, change in skin color, and shedding.

Sunburns

Your pig can get sunburnt if it is exposed to sunlight for too long. If they do they will get tired, weak, and even suffer from paralysis as well. Some can die due to heatstroke while other pigs can recover as well. You can ask your vet to provide a lotion, something like a sun block, for your pet.

Kidney and Bladder Disorders

Pigs can often face kidney and bladder problems due to a number of reasons; here are the following reasons behind the cause.

Cystitis

Cystitis is another word used to define inflammation of the bladder. This can cause pain, discomfort, and even stones.

Urolithiasis

Urolithiasis has to do with the bladder and kidneys as well. This term is used for the formation of stones which are created or deposited in the two organs. This is also known as calculi, the term used for stone. In pot bellied pigs, calculi can be found under the urethra and bladder in many cases. This is very painful and can cause concerns such as problems while passing urine, blood in urine, and pain. Both cystitis and urolithiasis are interlinked, and are commonly found in both male and female pigs.

Signs also include the pet frequently passing urine or trying to pass urine; this can be diagnosed through a urine test. Antibiotics and vaccines can be administered to flush the stones out of the body. If the stones are too large to be passed out through the stool and the anus, surgery will be required.

Psychogenic Polydipsia

Often, pigs can consume more water than their body needs, leading to Psychogenic Polydipsia. In order to check this, your vet will need your pet's urine sample. However, do not give your pig anything to eat for 12 hours before the test. During this fast, the pig can consume food but not water. Salt poisoning can also be a reason behind this disorder.

Who can cure the Pet Pigs?

Just like how you need to visit the doctor when you get sick, your pet animal needs to visit the veterinary specialist, or vet. A vet is a specialist in animal care, they are trained to treat and vaccinate all kinds of animals.

Treatment of your Pet Pot Bellied Pig

Vets can give your pet the needed vaccines, antibiotics, or the surgery it needs to get better. Daily checkups are the best way to prevent them from happening in the first place. Regular vaccinations will also help in keeping your pet pig safe from infections and diseases.

Duration of Treatment
Durations depend on the type of disease and surgery scars take a considerable time to heal. This is also dependant on how fast the disease or infection is, if it has just started or if it is severe.

Possible Outcomes
There are three possible outcomes, one being that your pet will be completely fine, two being that your pet is now fine but requires extra care as they have not fully recovered and may face lifelong problems. Thirdly, if the case is too advanced to treat, they may need to put the pig down.

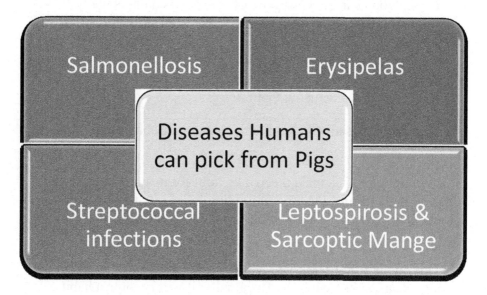

Bathing your Potbellied Pig
Pigs are naturally clean pets; it may seem hard to believe due to the mess they make especially in mud puddles, but they really are. You do not have to give your pet potbelly a bath every other day, once or twice a week is good enough. Too much bathing can cause its skin to dry out.

Bathing your pig may not be that easy either. If your pet pig enjoys the outdoors, set up a bath party in the yard by filling a pool, you can add toys in it too. If your pet likes the indoors, take it to the shower area. If you have issues in taking your pig in to the shower, you can try to trick it.

Cleaning the Eyes & Ears

Taking good care of your pet's eyes and ears daily is really important. Clean the area around the ears and eyes as regularly as you can to keep germs away. A brown discharge will be released. Use a damp and warm cloth to clean it. You can use the cloth to clean the ear as well; Q-tips are an option you can go for but be really careful while using them.

Tusks

If your pet pig is a male, keep a lookout for its tusks. They will need to be trimmed at a point in time. Do not do this on your own; let the vet take care of this.

Nose

This one is a bit tricky; you will actually need to fool your pet pig into cleaning its own nose. Eventually, it will become a habit.

Litter Box

Training your pig to take care of business is not easy. You will either have to hire a trainer to domesticate your pig and how to go in the litter box, and nowhere else. A young piglet can be trained easily. When your piglet grows older, it will not prefer using the litter box as it can not control when it has to go, and will take care of business when it is escorted outside. You can always consult a vet on this as well to give you ideas.

Trick:

Step 1- Fill a bowl with water.

Step 2- Add chopped carrots or apples so that they may sink to the bottom.

Step 3- The pig will blow bubbles and snorkel in order to get the carrots and apples

Step 4- Wipe the nose gently with a cloth or towel.

Dental Care

Potbellied pigs also need dental care just like you do. The newborn piglets need to have their teeth trimmed. They have 8 sharp teeth which are powerful enough to hurt their mother's tits while they are feeding, as well as hurt themselves as well. When they are 5-7 months old their adult teeth, known as canine teeth, will start to come out and replace their milking teeth. The canine teeth will eventually grow along with the pig throughout their lifetime and should be trimmed yearly.

This needs to be taken care of by professional vets as the pig will fight and may need to be anesthetized.

Adult potbellied pigs may get exposed tooth roots, which can be visibly seen coming out of the sides of their mouths. This is concerning and if your pot bellied is suffering from the same you should have an x-ray done to get the proper reason and diagnosis behind the abnormal growth.

Preventing Hazards

Keep small objects out of the way; keep toys but just not small ones. Train your pig to stay off the furniture. Add cushions in your pet's play room. Lastly, make or place ramps where there are stairs.

Chapter 7: Physical Characteristics

Potbellied pigs come in many colors and appearances. Although they are known for their bellies, there are many other breeds which look alike. Here are the physical characteristics of potbellied pigs:

Color

Potbellied pigs come in different colors depending on their breed. The colors depend on the breeding of the pig. Mixed breed potbellied pigs are of multiple colors, while pure bred pigs are of one color. These colors include:

Black

Brown

White

Light Pink

Black with Whites Stripes (Vice-Versa)

Black with White Spots (Vice-Versa)

Grey

Red

Did you know?

Owners love pigs as pets as they do not shed.

Height & Weight

The height and weight of the potbelly is a dependant factor. This is not only dependant of the diet or care of the pig; this also depends of the genes it got from the parents.

Length Measurement

If you want to measure the length of the pig, place a measuring tape on its head, and bring it down backwards to its tail. Do not measure the tail, measure till the base of the tail only. Tails are not a part of length measurement.

Girth Measurement

Take the girth measurement by placing the measurement tape around the pig's body behind the front legs.

X-Girth Measurement

In order to find this, multiply the girth measurement by itself. Let us assume your pig has a girth of 40. Multiply 40 or the number by itself. 40x40= 1600. Multiply this number with the length of the pig. Let us say that the length of the pig is 37 inches. This means you will multiply 1600 by 37. The total girth of the pig would be 59,200.

Weight Calculation

Divide the girth total by 400. 59,200 divided by 400 is 148. This is about the same amount of the accurate weight. There is a rough difference of 5 pounds from the accurate measurement in this method. So this means that the pig weighs in between 143-153 roughly.

Litter Size

The average size of the litter varies from 6-8 baby pigs. Sometimes, 8-10 piglets can be born as well. The delivery normally takes roughly 1.5-2 hours if there are no complications involved. It takes around 15 minutes to 30-35 minutes for each piglet to come out. Normal piglets will weigh from 6 to 12 ounces after birth.

Intelligence

The intelligence of your pet will leave your mind boggled. As a matter of fact, you will always have to be alert when you are around your pet as it monitors you and understands and communicates back. If the pig watches you opening cabinets and the refrigerator, it will not take long for it to open them as well.

Unlike dogs and cats, pigs can be trained with ease and in a short period of time. You can even teach your pet potbelly tips and tricks and watch everyone get amazed. They are social due to their personality, get along with other pets, and children too. They can even learn how to play video games as well!

Personality

Each piglet and adult pig has their own personality. The thing with pigs is that you can never tell how they will turn out to be. This depends on three factors, one being in the genes, two depending on the mood of the pig, and three, on you.

What you say or do also affects the pig and their nature. This is why you must keep your cool in all situations and not yell at the piglet or beat it. If so, it will learn to disobey you and the attitude will just get worse.

Did you know?

Pigs are number 4 in being the smartest animals. They come after Humans, Apes and Whales.

Heads Up

Just to stay on the clear side, it is important for you to know that some piglets are born with special needs; they may be abnormal from birth. This can also happen as they grow a bit older, as pigs can catch diseases which can lead to things like blindness, abnormal eating habits, and other noticeable symptoms.

Always keep in mind that it is not the potbellies' fault if it behaves in such a way. Do not scream at it, or even hit it. The pet should be taken to a vet immediately for proper treatment. The vet will give you good pointers which you can use to ensure your potbelly will recover, if there are chances for it to recover. At other times, the pet needs to be put to sleep as the diseases has spread out of control and is very dangerous.

Chapter 8: Naughty or Nice? Pigs and their Temperaments

All pigs differ in nature; some are more calm and obedient, whereas other pigs may be harder to handle.

If a pig feels it has not been getting enough care and attention it will start to act up. This includes not eating, nudging, not obeying you, refusing to play, etc.

If you have more than one pet, you may have to face a lot of drama as each pet wants to be their owner's favorite. If you own more than one pig, they will try to become the leader, and only one will succeed in that.

Male potbellied pigs are more stubborn compared to the females. If they are ignored they will get aggressive. Female potbellied pigs are less aggressive and calm, but during and after a pregnancy, they can become territorial, as all mothers tend to get.

As long as you play a lot with your potbelly, love and nurture it, give it treats, and yummy food, you shall have no complaints regarding their temperament.

Chapter 9: Reproduction & Breeding

Before you make your pet potbellied pigs mate, be careful and make sure the male is not aggressive. Aggressive male potbellied pigs do not make good mates or pets.

Breeding should be left to the professionals and not amateurs. If you are buying a piglet make sure it is from the litter that a professional breeder owns.

Female Potbellies

The female potbellies can start reproducing once they are 3 months old. If the pig fails to go into heat, it may be pregnant. This will most likely be the case if the female potbelly had a male potbelly as a companion in the same pen.

You can have the uterus and ovaries of your female potbellies removed via spaying. This can prevent them from getting aggressive and should be taken care of when the female pig is 3-6 months old.

If the female potbelly is expecting, she will give birth after 113 or 115 days for the babies to be born. During this time, the mother will start developing milk within her body to feed her piglets. The behavior of the mother will change as she is about to expect.

You can place a box in the yard where the mother can give birth. A soft blanket as bedding is good too; it should cover the entire area. The mother can give birth to 1 to 12 piglets at a time.

When the piglets start to make their way out, place them under a heat lamp as baby piglets cannot maintain temperatures of their bodies and will need the heat to feel warm. Make sure the lamp is not placed too close to the mother and her young as it can burn their skin.

Keep an eye on the piglets as they come; the mother can roll on top of her young by accident and smother them. This can be difficult to do, as the mother will feel very protective. After all the piglets have been born, make sure all of them have access to their mother's tits.

Male Potbellies
The males should be neutered when they are 2-3 months old. A 3 month old pig is mature enough to get a 3 month old female pig pregnant. The male pigs which are not neutered tend to be moody and aggressive. This is one of the main reasons they are not suitable as pets. The pigs which can mate should be kept in separate pens and should be properly fenced.

Newborn Potbellies
Newborn runts or piglets need complete access to their mother and her milk. The milk helps protect the young piglets against diseases. They need to feed off their mother for at least 4-5 minutes to have enough milk. Once the mother has no more left, she will produce more within an hour.

Lifespan
The average lifespan of a potbellied pig is between the ages of 15-20 years but it also depends on their diet and the vaccines they are administered. There is no scientific theory on this, but there are many factors which make this a depending factor. If the pig is getting a great diet, and is regularly taken to the vet, it will live longer than one which is on a poor diet and is likely to get infected with a life threatening disease.

Signs for Potbelly Pregnancy
As mentioned before, female potbellied pigs have a gestation period of 112 to 115 days. This can also be up to 3 months as well depending on the pregnancy. You will be able to tell if a potbelly is expecting if she fails to go into heat. To confirm the pregnancy, take her to the vet for an ultrasound.

While the pregnancy continues, her body will expand and drag towards the bottom and eventually, her teats will be at a point during the pregnancy, touching the ground. A week before the delivery, her vulva will swell, it is a sign that the delivery time is near. The milk will start to form in her body. The milk line will become visible along her teats. Towards the end, she will feel very restless and she will start nesting.

Premature Piglets

Take the premature piglet to the vet. Take the vet's advice on the baby. Keep one thing in mind as well, some normal piglets will need to be bottle fed; such piglets either do not have access to their mother's teats or do not know what to do. This does not mean the piglet is abnormal or premature.

Piglet Sight

Baby pigs are able to see as soon as they are born. Their vision will not be as good but their sense of smell will be sharp, which helps them make their way around. Some piglets do not smell or see properly as they are more dependant on the mother. This can be due to the afterbirth sac as well. It will come off by itself but if it does not, gently peel it off *carefully*.

Chapter 10: Habitat

The natural habitat for potbellied pigs is the great outdoors since they are quite energetic animals. However, what you have to make sure is that no matter inside or out, the premises should be pig-proof to ensure your potbellied pigs remain healthy and happy.

Living Outdoors

Many pet owners, especially owners of potbellied pigs, prefer their pets outside their house, in the front or back yard. This is due to a lot of factors.

- Pigs love to get dirty.
- Pigs need open space to play and grow.
- Pigs are fond of the outdoors comparatively.
- Pigs grow more in their 'natural' habitat.

Although many prefer their pet pigs outside, there are some precautions which must be taken.

Climate & Temperature

Since pigs cannot sweat, their bodies can get easily overheated, but they can also lose the heat when it becomes too chilly outside for them. You must maintain a daily temperature check; if it is too hot or too cold outside, do not let them out.

Precautions you must take!

The more space you have, the better it is for the pet. Pigs love to run around but to ensure your pig stays safe, you must take a few precautions.

First things first, you will need to make a small house or shelter for them; something like a dog house, but bigger and wider. It has to be very sturdy with no splinters sticking out or nails to ensure your pig does not get injured while in it. It also has to be rainproof so that your pet can remain warm and cozy during those wet and cold days.

Place bedding or a blanket to help the potbelly feel comfortable and warm. The more comfortable the pet is, the more it will love its habitat. Remove the bedding if it gets too hot for your pet pig so that it doesn't get overheated. Straw is a good alternative to consider.

Did You know?

Many pet owners are unaware that pigs sweat through their noses. The tiny droplets which can be seen on the nose are sweat drops.

Make sure your pigs have access to a water source 24/7. In the summer time, you may want to consider keeping a small kiddy pool for them to cool off in as they need to keep their temperatures low. The pigs will try to find mud to cool off if they are unable to find cool water. Clean their drinking water often as they will love to make it dirty, and it will not take them long.

If you have a male potbelly that is able to mate, you will need to keep it fenced up. When male pigs are in heat they tend to get aggressive and ignore commands. If you want your pig or pigs to mate, keep them within a sturdy fence in one area of the yard or field.

Pigs love to dig and they have a very keen sense of smell so you may want to keep all your flower beds away from their enclosure. Consider it this way; your pig will dig its way half way across the world in order to follow the scent it picked up. You may also want to fence the ground; they can escape by digging their way through the bottom.

Quick Summary
Here are the things you need to keep in mind to ensure your pot belly pig remains healthy.

- Keep an eye on the temperature.

- Make sure their bedding is dry and warm and does not get wet.

Living Indoors

Pigs are not used to living indoors; they prefer open spaces, freedom to run, chase, play, etc. In order to get your potbelly to adjust to the indoors, you will have to train it. Remember that young potbellies are easy to train, but as they grow older its best to hire a professional to train them.

Training

You will need to train your piglet or adult pig to adjust in your home. Your pig must learn to stay off the furniture, behave and obey, not make a mess of things, get along with other pets, and family.

> **Tip:** When your pigs obey a command, give it a treat such as apples grapes, and carrots to motivate its behaviour.

Another very important thing you must keep in mind is that your pet will need to take care of business and this can happen any time of day. Take your piglet outside every once in a while so that it knows it cannot relieve itself indoors. As the piglet matures, it will wait to go until escorted outside. You can also make a small piggy door in your front door so it may come and go whenever it wants to.

Pigs are like toddlers, they will take literally anything and everything in their mouths and this is why you must make sure there are no items within the house which it can choke on. Another important thing you must remember is that your pig will try to nibble or chew its way through all of the electric chords in your house. You can either rearrange the wiring so that your pig cannot place the wires in its mouth or use really fat or chew free chords.

Space

In order to properly grow, your pig needs all the space it can get. This is one of the main reasons why most pet pig owners prefer to keep their pets outside.

A closet, the basement, or a small storage room is good enough for your pet. Place comfortable bedding within the room. Avoid sleeping bags; pigs do not like them at all. Go for straw or rags, they prefer them more as well as pillows and blankets. Avoid placing furniture in the room; they will hurt themselves by jumping on and off it.

Getting Bored

Pigs can get bored if they are left alone or kept inside for too long. Place toys within the room to keep it stimulated. Take it outside for an hour or so at least once a day. Exercise will allow it to stay fit and to grow properly. Bored pigs will get lazy which is not healthy for them at all. A bored and lonely pig will chew on your carpet, make a mess, jump on your bed and sofa, and it will even try to ruin your perfect wall. Many pigs even nudge their owners as well as a way of letting them know they want attention.

You need to outsmart your pet pig; they will do anything to make a mess, and if they do, good luck cleaning it all up.

Did you know?

Your pig will actually open your refrigerator if it is bored or hungry.

Avoiding Injuries

Pigs are very smart and can open cabinets and even your refrigerator with ease. You will need to place locks on all the cabinets and make sure all sprays, cleaners, acids, etc are locked away in a high place so that your pig cannot get to them at all. Install ramps where you want the pet to have access, like from the bedroom into the main hall. Their short legs are not built for climbing stairs after all.

Chapter 11: Training your Potbelly

Pigs are quick learners but that's not always a good thing. You have two options you can go for which are:

- Professional Training

- Self Training

Professional Training
You can ask your local vet or a family member or even a friend for the trainer who trained their pet. Since pigs are very unique pets, it will be a bit hard to find a professional trainer, but it is not impossible. You can find some online but make sure you check up on them by asking for referrals or talking with some of their past clients.

The trainer will teach your potbelly how to obey you and follow the house rules. They will also guide you on how you can make your pig obey your commands. The professional trainer can and will answer all the questions you have related to the training. Here are a few you should ask.

Questions you should ask the Trainer
1. How long have you been training pet pigs?
2. Do you have any certificates in training animals?
3. Do you have certificates in training pigs?
4. How are pigs different from other animals?
5. Do they require extra special training?
6. How can I make my pet potbelly obey me?
7. Will it obey only me?
8. Will it refuse to obey me?
9. What if it stops obeying me?

10. Which techniques can I use with my pig?

You need to let your pig know who's boss and the answers to the abovementioned questions will help you do that.

Self Training

A lot of pet owners do not want professional pig trainers to train their pigs. This will require a lot of hard work and dedication. Training a pet pig is no joke at all. In order to train one, you must research their behavior and think like a pig as well. No, seriously!

The Harness

Keep in mind that a harness should not be just be used to keep your pig tethered and prevent it from wandering off. The main purpose is to keep it safe and let it know you mean it no harm.

There are two types of training harnesses which you can use.

Type A Harness

This harness can be easily slipped on to your pet pig by moving it over its head and by snapping it shut between the legs.

Type B Harness

This harness has two locks, one that goes around the neck of the pig and the second between the legs.

Why use the Harness in Training?

Some piglets and pigs do not like human contact at all. This is because they are afraid that you may try or actually harm them. They will not let you come near them let alone touch or rub their bellies. You need to encourage your pig to socialize, which is where the harness comes in. The harness will keep the pig by your side and allow it to feel secure. Once it relaxes, you can stop using the harness.

Starting Harness Training

Always remember the first step of the harness training; never ever force your pig into the harness. You can trick it, but never force it or else it will never trust it.

Once you have tricked the pig into the harness, do not pick it up immediately. Slowly pick up your pig and move around. The pig will try to jump off so maintain a strong grip and hold on to it.

If the pig is still upset and uncomfortable, offer it more food. If that does not work, place the pig back down gently and open the harness, and say 'go,' 'you are free,' 'have fun,' any phrase you want.

Keep talking to your pig in a soothing voice to make sure it remains calm. Even if you are adjusting the harness, tell your potbelly that you are not going to harm it; you are just fixing the harness. While doing so, pat the pig, make it calm down, talk to it, use phrases like 'ok boy', 'easy there', 'that's a good boy' or 'hey girl', 'stay calm, 'good girl, 'who is a good girl.'

Step two will start once your pig has been harnessed. Pigs are not fond of being in a harness for too long and may start to get restless after a while.

First thing you should do is let the pig wander around for a bit; do not apply pressure or pull back on the harness abruptly. Once the pig calms down, call out its name. Do not pull on the leash too hard; a little pressure will be enough to let it know you mean business. Pull the leash and yell 'hold' when you want it to stop moving, let go a bit and say 'go' or 'walk' when you want it to move. Practice this for a couple of days on a regular basis until the pig starts responding.

A time will come when it will realize it has to stay near you and you are not trying to harm it. You can teach your pet pig how to go on walks this way too without fearing it might bolt.

> **Trick:** Trick your pig in to the harness by luring it with food. The pig will come towards the harness, and you can place it on instantly without alarming it.

Training your Pig to Socialize

First thing you need to do is take your pig out and let it play with other animals. Do not leave your pig alone with your pet dogs, unless they have been trained to behave around your pet pot bellies.

Do not yell at your pig or talk in a loud voice. Your pet pig is sensitive when it comes to such things and will not tolerate this behavior. Do not blame it for gobbling up something you left outside for it to find, or for making a mess. Instead, train it so that it does not make that mistake.

The breeder you purchased your pet from or the owner should have other pig pets or other animals as pets. If not, the first step you need to follow is making the pig used to your company. The harness training is the answer to that. Once the pig feels secure around your company, it will have no problems in adjusting to others as well.

Do not pick your pig up or let others handle it too often. This will make them feel uneasy and they will not be able to socialize well either.

Never force your pig into doing something it does not want to do. Use words and phrases for activities they do, if they disobey you, use words like 'no' or 'down.' When they stop, use positive words like 'good'

You can use terms like 'sorry' to apologize to your pig if they are hurt or express your affection by saying 'I love you' or 'love you, love ya.' Always remember to use one specific word or phrase only.

Potty Training- Indoors and Out

Potty training has always been the most important and concerning thing for pet owners. No one wants their pets to take care of business anywhere; imagine how angry someone would be if they accidently sat or stepped on your pets unpleasant gift. You do not have to worry much about your pet potbelly in this regard though. You can train your pet to go outside as well as at a particular place in your home as well.

> **Tip :** It is always a good idea to place a litter box within the house as well as outside for your pet potbelly

Indoor Potty Training

Like any other pet owner, you would want your pet to go outside to relieve itself. However, in order for them to do that, they need proper training, but some prefer inside. The litter box training is not that difficult, but it will take a few days for your pet to get used to that potty routine.

First things first, training piglets aged 6 months or younger is easier than potty training adult pigs. However, do keep in mind that they may not be able to control themselves sometimes.

Keep a litter box in the corner of your house. Make sure your pet can access the box whenever it needs to go. Take them towards the box every hour or so, so that they can go themselves.

Do not give your pet any treats during this training session even if they did a good job. Giving treats will make your pet want to go over and over again since it will not know any better. They should pick this up within a week, and during that duration, do not change the position of the litter box; you pig has to be trained to go towards one spot only.

Most pigs prefer going about their business during the night, when no one is looking and with more space to comfortably get their business done with.

Make sure the pet is not familiar with the entire house yet as it will wander all around, break things, and leave smelly 'presents' for you around the house.

Going Outside

Take your pig outside every 1-2 hours for the potty and make this their daily routine. Your pet pig will eventually realize that it will need to go outside if it needs to relieve itself. Do not feed your pet treats if it goes outside for this; it will pretend that it needs to 'go' jus to get them then!

Rooting

Pigs love to dig around. Rooting is a term used to describe digging. This is a very natural behavior in all pigs, but for owners, this can get quite annoying. Pigs have a keen sense of smell, and even if they are left inside, they will not fight this instinct. They will go through your cabinets, fridge, entire room and kitchen if they have to.

In order to stop this from becoming a big issue as the pet grows older, you will need to train it to behave properly. Do not discourage your pet from rooting in the yard or outside your house. You can add restrictions on your pet inside, but not too much. Discouraging them from following their instincts for too long might make them depressed.

In order to keep your pet happy, place old rags and unwanted or unneeded blankets in its room it can root through. If your pet pig nudges your ankles it is trying to indicate that it is hungry. However, this is not acceptable behavior; it may even get aggressive if it is not discouraged.

Do not feed your pig if it behaves in such a manner. Your pet must understand that this behavior will not be tolerated and if it wants to eat, it has to wait until it is meal time.

Scratching

Pigs naturally have dry and itchy skin. They will try to scratch themselves with whatever they can find. This is why they are fond of rubbing their bodies on rough surfaces. This is not a healthy habit though. Unfortunately, rubbing themselves on rough surfaces will just ruin its skin making it itchier so keep it away from it. While you are at it, do not give your pig a bath if they are facing such a problem. The best solution for a scratchy pig is moisturizing lotion and ensuring it stays away from such surfaces.

Did You Know?

Since they have dry and itchy skin, pigs love having their bellied rubbed

Biting and Aggressive Behavior

Pigs are naturally territorial and will also get jealous if their owner's attention is diverted from them. They may even get aggressive if they are ignored for too long.

Biting

The pig will chomp on your furniture and other items around your home if it is left unsupervised or untrained. That's because they are ALWAYS hungry! A healthy diet will ensure your pot belly pig remains satiated and happy.

Aggression

A pig can get aggressive due to a number of reasons as we discussed before. However, if you fail to keep your anger in check when they do act out, your pot belly's aggression will take a turn for the worst. If your pet is behaving in such a way, it could be because it is sick, hungry, or is not getting enough attention. Often male potbellies show more aggression than female potbellies.

Territorial Pigs

Pigs are very territorial and will mark their territory to keep other pigs away. This is not a healthy habit and must be overcome as soon as possible. This includes the mother's behavior towards her young. Even though she is familiar with you, she will not like you anywhere near her piglets.

If you wish to overcome such a problem, separate the pigs from the aggressive ones. It will placate the pigs who do not get along.

Wallowing

Wallowing is necessary for pigs as it allows them to cool off and maintain a healthy body temperature. In order for them to stay cool during really hot and dry weather, you will need to ensure they have access to water. Place a small pool near their room, so that they can wallow in it to prevent issues like overheating and sunburns. Keep the pool water clean, and change it as often as needed. Pigs prefer mud sometimes as well, but to keep their wallowing mess free, use water instead.

Chapter 12: Getting a Companion for Piggie

Your pot belly pig can get lonely if it does not have a companion. This is why many owners opt for another pet pig. There is one thing you must remember first. Your pet pig might not get along with its new companion. This can be due to many reasons; the first may feel insecure regarding your affections and if it is territorial, it will definitely not want another pig around. Bringing up both pigs together as piglets cannot ensure they will get along as they grow older.

How to introduce a new Pig(s)

The first step you must take when introducing two pigs is supervising them. Monitor the behavior of your older pet, try to figure out if they are getting along with each other. Try to make them come in front of each other slowly, keep them in separate pens or keep a baby gate between them for a few days and note how they react.

Then, once you think they are ready to meet each other officially, open the pen or gate and let them interact. If the introduction is successful, let both stay in the same pen or the same side of the room. If not, keep them apart, and then reintroduce them after another couple of days.

Within a few weeks, the fighting pigs should begin to settle down. During this duration, steadily increase their interaction with each other. The more they will see each other, the better it will be.

If they start fighting, break it up. Keep your pet in the harness during the meet; since you have already trained it to listen to you through the harness training, it will help you restrain it if a fight breaks out.

While introducing the pigs, you need to make sure they are of the same age, height, and weight too. Adult pigs and piglets may not get along unless they are parent and child. The adult pig will harm the piglet if it feels territorial.

If the pigs behave well during the interaction, do not reward them; they will pretend to be comfortable with each other just so that they can get more. On the other hand, if your older pet pig behaves badly, do not punish it. This can cause a bitterer side of the pig to come out towards the new pet. Never hit the pig, it will make it more stubborn, especially if it is a baby.

The best thing to do before you buy a new pet is to introduce your pet pig to other pigs. See how the pet behaves around them. If the interaction is positive, you can definitely think about getting another pet. If not, then give your pig more time to adjust.

Chapter 13: License, & Insurance

It is important to be updated about all the laws regarding pets within the country in which you reside. Make sure you have required information if you are allowed to keep a pet pig in the country you reside in. If so, here is what you will need to know regarding the cost of buying a potbellied pig, if you require a license for one, if insurance is needed, and how to purchase one.

Cost of a Potbellied Pig in the United States

The cost of the pet depends on many factors. If the pig is a potbelly which has been raised on a farm, its price will be different from a pig which has been raised by a breeder. The average range of a potbelly pig is between $300- $ 1,000. If the pigs are neutered, vaccinated, well fed and bred, they will cost more.

Cost of a Potbellied Pig the United Kingdom

The same stays true for the United Kingdom as well. The price of a pet potbelly depends on how old the pig is, if it is vaccinated, and who has raised the pet until that point. On average, the pet costs between £50- £150. This excludes transport cost as well as food and toys cost.

Purchasing a Pig in the United States

Look for a relative, friend, or a breeder who wants to put a potbellied pig up for adoption. After that, be sure to ask the questions we have discussed before. If the breeder or friend states the pig has been vaccinated and asks for a high price, make sure to ask them about the certificates. If the pig has not been vaccinated do not pay them such a high amount. Settle the amount after all the questions have been answered so that you don't end up paying more than what the pig's worth.

Purchasing a Pig in the United Kingdom

The same goes for the United Kingdom. Adopt a pig from a breeder, pet store, friend or relative. Be sure to ask all the information needed regarding the adoption. Ask for all the documents as well.

License in the United States

It is necessary to get your pet licensed. According to the act of Racine Municipal Code, all domestic pets must be licensed. These include cats, dogs, ferrets and potbellied pigs. This license helps the authorities to identify your pet pig in case it gets lost. The license also keeps track of all the health related medical files, including vaccines and vet visits.

It can cost you $11.00 to get your pig licensed. Plus, only 3 domestic animals and 2 per family are allowed in the US. If owners have more than 3 pets and reside in a single family residence, they will need the Pet Fancier's Permit, but, only one potbellied pig will be allowed to them.

License in the United Kingdom

Yes, you must get your pet pig registered and receive a license stating that the registration has been completed. The National Pig Identification and Tracking System known as NPITS is an operation which came forth in 2002. According to NPITS, all pigs must be registered for a license.

Anyone who wants to go forth with the adoption must sign a form called the Pig Herd Application Form. You can take a look at the Pig Welfare Requirements Booklet as well to ensure you have taken all measures to prepare yourself to adopt a pig. You can even call CPH and register your pig by calling 0845 603 7777.

Walking License
Yes, you will require a walking license as well in order to take the pet pig outside on walks. If you reside outside the United Kingdom, you must send a photo copy to the nearby local police station as well.

Insurance for Potbellied Pigs
The insurance will help you cover medical costs if your pet gets into any mishaps and accidents or requires surgery.

What is Insurance?
Insurance is a policy through which owners of pets can cover their pet's medical charges and responsibilities. Though pigs are considered as pets, they are not as popular as other domestic pets such as a cat or a dog. This is why it will take a bit of homework to find the right firm which provides insurance for your pet.

Potbelly Insurance
Potbellied pigs are famous as pets, so finding insurance for them will not be difficult and will be quite necessary. The potbellied pig can weigh up to 500 pounds. Trimming the tusks, vaccinations, neutering, all of this can cost you a lot. The insurance plan will help cut these down so that you can easily afford to get it vaccinated and ensure it remains disease free.

Companies Providing Insurance
There are 3 companies which provide insurance for potbellied pigs in the United States. These include:

- Pet Assure Pet Insurance

- VPI Pet Insurance

- Lester Kalmanson Agency Inc.

The company which provides pet insurance in the United Kingdom is:

- Exotic Direct

Birth Marks & Tattoos
If your potbelly pig has marks or tattoos on its body, you must include this information in the registry as well. These will help identify it if it gets lost.

Chapter 14: Adoption & Abandonment

Adoption

So you decided to adopt a potbellied pig as a pet. Great idea, indeed these cute little angels make great pets. Make sure you have acquired all the knowledge required, and have taken all measures necessary in order to continue with the procedure.

Make sure you go online and do your bit of research and homework as well. Learning from other's experience will help you in raising your own potbellied pig. Take all the time you need in preparing and do not just scan through.

Adoption from Breeder

As mentioned previously, make sure you are completely satisfied with the breeder, the health of the piglet, and that the breeder is a professional.

Adoption from Sanctuaries

Adopting a pig or piglet from a sanctuary is always a good idea as well. You can search online for the closest sanctuary or take a look at the list of those given in this book.

The procedure is simple, once you know you are ready to adopt, call them to attain all the needed information, and then visit their website to fill the adoption form. Some forms can be filled online whereas other forms will need to be printed and then personally submitted.

It is always a good idea to visit the sanctuary personally to see what kind of environment they offer their pigs and how they take care of them. Personal satisfaction is necessary while adopting from sanctuaries as well.

Once the form has been filled, a small background check will also be conducted. This includes an interview which the supervisor of the agency will have with you. If they think you are ready and you are eligible to adopt, they will introduce you to the pigs, where you can select the one you want to take home with you.

Questioning

Ask the representatives questions as well. Be prepared to answer a few yourself. Since many sanctuaries have abandoned pigs, they will be thorough in determining whether you will be a good owner to them. Once they see you are actually serious about the adoption process, only then will you be granted permission to adopt.

Abandonment

Unfortunately, hundreds of pigs are abandoned each year. There can be many reasons behind this. The owner was told the pig will not grow past a certain height and weight, but it did, leading to abandonment. Pet pigs with voracious appetites and those with aggressive demeanors also number among these.

There are several reasons why owners decide to abandon their pet potbellied pigs, but the main question is that why do they leave them helpless and left alone to die? Those pigs are faced with serious malnutrition problems and can easily catch diseases which can make them seriously ill. Sadly, most are put to sleep.

Sanctuaries

The best option is to either give your pet pig away to another owner who is willing to take care of it in a proper manner and is serious about the adoption. Another option would be to place the abandoned pig within a sanctuary.

This is actually a preferred option for many as the staff there are trained and know how to take care of the pigs, how to train them, provide them with the proper diet and nutrition requirements and give them the needed medication and vaccines on time.

You cannot just drop your pig off in front of the sanctuary; you must first research it online. Once you have done that, you will find a form, commonly known as the 'release form'. Fill it and send it for the procedure to be completed. Once the form has gone forward, the representatives of the sanctuary will contact you, and will conduct a small interview with you. This interview will consist of why you want to abandon your pet, if the pet is up to date on its vaccine, which diet has been given to them till date, etc.

Once the representatives are satisfied that you can no longer take care of the pet, they will take care of all the legal processing, and you will be free from the ownership of the potbellied pig.

Bordering & Fostering

Many owners have unconditional love and find it extremely hard to let go of their pets when it comes to giving them up. This is why some sanctuaries can take care of your potbellied pig temporarily. In this foster care, your pet will be looked after properly, will be given all medical vaccinations, and will be sent into another home to a family who is willing to adopt it. This will give the previous owners the satisfaction that their pet is in good hands. The pet pig might be sent to a temporary home, but not for adoption purposes. This is known as bordering.

In bordering, the pet will be under the care of the sanctuary until you come back to fetch it. This option is the best one for those pet owners who cannot stand seperating from their pets. This is mostly temporary though, until the owner has taken care of business.

Do keep in mind that not all of the sanctuaries offer this option to pet owners. Since there are just a few sanctuaries which offer such aid and assistance, you will have to take out time to find the right one that does.

Help Out

You can always help out the sanctuaries as well. There are three ways in which you can do that. First is to volunteer and spend time in helping to raise the pigs. The second method is to give the sanctuary charity or donations; this will help them keep up with the costs of feeding the pigs as well as give them medical aid. The third way is to sponsor them. If you own a small food store, or a pharmacy, you can give a small amount in the beginning or end of each month to pitch in and help out.

Chapter15: Finding the Perfect Sanctuary

Finding the perfect sanctuary is no joke; your pet potbelly's health is on the line, which means you cannot just give up on it like it never existed. Giving up on your pet is like taking a part of you and giving it away; it is painful, but at times it is for the best as well.

This is why you must ensure that the sanctuary in which you are giving your potbellied pig to is proper, legal, and will be able to take good care of it, the kind which your pet requires. Your potbelly has been with you for quite some time now, which means you understand your pet unlike anyone else. This also means that you must find other people who can understand the needs and wants of the pet as well.

Research
In order for you to find the appropriate sanctuary, you must first do a lot of research. Remember, your pet has been a huge part of your life and it is never easy to let go, which is why you must analyze every aspect of the process of abandonment for your pet's best interest.

Search online about the sanctuary which is close to your home, this way you will always feel like your pet is close by. Once you have chosen the desired sanctuary, do some extensive research about them online. View blogs and forums about the sanctuary, and see if other pet owners are satisfied with the care they are giving to their potbelly. Do not just scan through the first couple of pages and forums you see. You must go in deep.

Comparison
Once you are fairly satisfied, the next step for you will be to compare the sanctuaries. Comparison is always a good idea,

often; we fail to see that another place can be giving our pets a better way of life, as many of us also go towards the first option given to us.

Once you find a satisfactory sanctuary, you can move on to the next step.

Policies

Make sure you have taken a good and a very careful look at the policy of the sanctuary. Each sanctuary has its own, which is why during the comparison phase this is necessary.

When you have read each and every clause, and have understood it, it's time to take a road trip.

Plan a Visit

Now, your step is to plan a small visit to the sanctuary; you do not have to take your pet along, but it is up to you, as the pig may want to explore the environment as well. Surprise visits are always a good idea too, it depends if they are allowed though. Once you have reached, take a tour around and about the sanctuary. Learn how they take care of the pet, how they treat the pets, and how they prepare the pet to adapt to a new environment.

Ask them questions as well; ask them about every little thing you can come up with. This will not just satisfy the concerns you have towards the pet, but you will figure out if your pet is better off in the selected sanctuary.

Plan Trip Number 2

Now it's time to plan the second trip to the sanctuary, but not the one you selected. This time, you will visit another one. Go through the same procedure as you did with the first trip. Make it unexpected, take a grand tour, and satisfy your inner motherhood, after all, your pet is more or less like a child to you.

Pet's Trip

Now take your potbellied pig to the sanctuary that you thought was best. Let it roam around a bit, and let it observe the environment as well. Remember what we said about pigs having a great sense of smell? They are great at sensing emotions as well, so if your pig is not happy it can be either of two reasons. One, it senses that you are leaving it, which is why it is afraid to let you go, secondly, the new environment is making it uncomfortable, for which it will need time to adapt.

Visits

Some sanctuaries do not allow it, but you can visit the pig every now and then just to make sure it is doing as fine as you had expected. Sanctuaries sometimes approve of this as it becomes hard for pigs to let go of their owner after being attached to them. You may be granted permission to view your pet from far away, or you will not get approval at all.

Questions

Do not hesitate at all when it comes to asking questions. You have every right to ask any kind and number you want to, these questions can be from the following as well.

List of Questions

Will my Pet Adapt to a new Environment Easily?

This actually depends on the pet itself and the environment too. If the pet adapted to you, your family, and your household with ease, it will adapt to another as well. This depends on the environment tool; there will be other pigs at the sanctuary, so it truly depends on how social your pet is. If the pet is able to go along with the crowd, it's good, but if it does not blend will, there will be a few concerns. The people at the sanctuary will teach it how to become open to other potbellies.

Will its Diet be taken care of appropriately?

The workers at the sanctuary have worked with many pigs prior to yours; this means they know exactly what they are doing. This also means that they know what the requirements of your pet are, and they will make sure to keep it on the diet it previously was on. There will be no compromises on the health of your pet potbelly.

What about Medical Care?

The main purpose of the sanctuaries is to give your potbelly a home, love and unconditional and irrevocable care. All of the pig's medical needs will be taken care of. The sanctuaries have in-house vets who will be looking after the pet almost 24/7, which means you will not have to worry about the vaccinations of the pet.

Will the Potbelly be bred?

No, these potbellies are not mated with each other. It is already hard to take care of the thousands of abandoned pigs, there is no need for them to extend their family with litters. If the potbellied pig is not neutered or spayed, they will be once they come to the sanctuary. This will make sure that they do not produce babies, and they will not be difficult to control during mating season.

How can I rest assure that my pig is in good hands?

Well to be honest, there is no real way to ensure your pig is in safe hands. You can always plan visits and meet the pig. It will satisfy you, or you can ask a friend or relative who works there to update you. You can even volunteer there yourself if the sanctuary allows it so that you can be completely satisfied from all aspects.

Will I have to pay?

This depends, if you are leaving the pig behind for good, or if you are leaving it in their care for a short period of time. If yes, you will be told before letting go of your pet. Each sanctuary has its own set of rules; this depends on the preferred sanctuary as well.

Questions to Expect

You will be asked a lot of questions as well; this is going to be the interview phase during the abandonment process. The representative will ask you all sorts of questions to ensure that you have no other choice but to give up on your pet. The following are some you need to be prepared for:

Questions to be prepared for

Why are you abandoning the Pet?

Until and unless you have a very valid and truly appropriate reason to let go of the pet, you will not be allowed to give up on it. If according to the board of the sanctuary, your reason is legit, they will accept it and the process will move on. There can be many reasons to support the pet's abandonment, such as financial crisis, or unexpected pig growth, or aggressive behavior.

Will you adopt the Pig once again if your Financial Condition Improves?

Give an honest reply, if you do not want to adopt it again, clearly say no and tell them why. If you say yes, let them know this is only temporary and that you are willing to take your pet back after your condition has stabilized.

There can be many reasons for saying no, but do clarify. One of the backup reasons can be because this crisis may happen again due to the sort of business you are in, and it will be too painful for you as it is of now. Another backup reason could be that you cannot afford one in the future either.

Has the potbelly received all its vaccinations till date?

Once again, stay honest. If it has been vaccinated, show them the medical reports and the proof as well. If not, tell them you have not given it its required shots due to a certain reason, and then explain.

Does the Pet have any Serious Medical Conditions?

If the pig does, accept it. You should not put other potbellied pigs in danger just because you need a shelter for your own. Pigs carry viruses and diseases which are contagious. If it is very serious, the pig may need to be euthanized.

Is the Pet trained?

This helps the sanctuary know if the potbelly is capable of interacting and adapting to a new environment. If you have trained the pet, it has better chances of adapting and being social to the other pigs, especially if it has been trained to adapt with other pets. If not, the volunteers and the staff at the respected sanctuary will train it.

Is the Pet Abnormal?

Sometimes, the behavior of the pet can be deemed unacceptable. This can be due to two reasons, one being that the pig has a genetic abnormality, and it has been either genetic, or it got it as it grew up. The second reason for such a behavior is the attitude and nature of the pig. If is rare to see, but some pigs are not social or adaptable at all.

Other Questions

In order to meet their satisfaction, the sanctuary can, and will ask you questions of all sorts. This includes many other questions such as where did you adopt the pet from? Why did you adopt it? etc.

Chapter16: Cost & Expenses

The monthly and yearly expense of your pet potbelly depends on a couple of factors such as age, height, health, parents, etc. A piglet potbelly has different needs, so compared to an adult or teenage potbelly, its expenses will vary.

Annual Expense

The annual expense also depends on various factors. Here are tables to help you out.

	Initial Costs		Annual Costs
Spay/ Neuter/Shots	$250-$500 £160-£256	**Feed**	$1,000 £640
Fencing	$500-$1,000 (By Professionals) £256-£640	**Vet Care**	$750-$1,200 £481-£770
		Medical Care	$5,000 £3200
Storages & Sheds	$350-$500 £224-£288	**Travelling**	$50/ Day £32/ Day
Pool & Water Dish	$200 £125	**Supplies**	$500 £256
Crates & Ramps	$500-$750 £256-£481	**Average Annual Costs**	$1,000-$1,500 £640-£962
Toys & Sand Pile	$200 £128		

Toys

Toys are a great way to keep your potbelly busy and help your pet learn. You can teach tricks and commands to your pets with the busy ball such as 'Catch' or 'Go'.

Let your potbelly enjoy the cool water against its skin in a kiddy pool. This will not just keep the temperature low; it will also please the potbelly as well. You can get your pet some nice chew toys as well. Pigs have sharp teeth and powerful jaws which are not suitable for all kinds of toys, but they will enjoy chew toys for sure.

Health Expenses

Piglets can catch genetic diseases from one another while in the womb. If the father was infected, the disease will also be carried to the mother through sexual contact, which will then transfer into the piglet.

Some piglets tend to get a hold of viruses and diseases as they are growing up. This may not be genetic, but it is easy for them to get infected throughout any phase of their lives.

The kind of infections and diseases they get is dependent on their diets and health as well, including daily activities. Depending on the infection or disease, the vet will conduct the treatment. The cost will vary, but if the pet is taken to the vet every now and then for vaccinations, this can be prevented from occurring in the first place.

This will even save you thousands of dollars; also the pet potbelly will not have to be put to sleep if the disease is that bad.

Damages

Pigs are extremely curious creatures. They love to experiment around the household, play, and break things as well. They do not deliberately do this, but this is just how are they are derived, or programmed.

They can cause the household and the property many forms of damage. This includes breaking in to the refrigerator, ripping clothes, breaking furniture, and even hurting themselves.

Furniture Damages

Pigs love to make a mess of things; they also love to entertain themselves, no matter what the consequences may be. They can end up breaking not just the furniture, but their bones as well. This includes fractures, and fatal falls as well. Pigs will love to turn your furniture into their own personal playground. They will jump on your couch, break your favorite lamp, even the antique vase you have in your sitting room. That's not all; they will not even spare your bedroom either.

Their mischief will be fun for them, but you are the one who will have to pay for the broken wood and bones. This is why it is important to pig-proof the entire house, not just so that you can save money and your furniture, but also to ensure that your pet remains safe as well.

Food Damages

It sounds quite funny when you tell someone that your pig can actually open the refrigerator, or when you hear something like this too. It is quite true; pigs are actually smart enough to do that. Piglets, from a very small age can pick up everything they see. If they are hungry, and they see you opening the fridge, taking out food, they will know that from now onwards, they do not need to be dependent on you for food, when they can open it and get it themselves.

This will create a huge mess in the kitchen, and that is not all, a lot of food will go to waste as well. Pigs love to eat, but they will not be able to finish every single thing they start on if they have many options to pick from. This can waste food, and this also means that you will have to go grocery shopping, again.

Cabinets and Storages

Your potbelly is not just smart enough to open refrigerators, it can also easily open draws, cabinets, and storage places as well. As mentioned before, potbellies have a great sense of smell, and a very sharp and keen one too. This makes it easy for them to detect any food and edibles lying around the house, unless you hide them in the attic that is. In order to prevent the chaos from occurring, hide the food on shelves and cabinets which are high above the ground so that the potbellied pig cannot reach it at all.

Other Damages

Pigs have sharp teeth and love to tear their way into many things. This includes clothes, toys, and anything they can access. Make sure you train your potbelly not to do this; it will be hard to train an adult potbelly, but not so hard with a piglet. Plus make sure if you do not give them anything valuable or expensive to play with.

Fencing and Penning

Often, male potbellies, and sometimes the female potbelly need to be fenced up. There can be many reasons behind this, like the male's behavior, mating purposes, or if your pig resides outside of the household residence. You will need to make sure the pigs are secured, and that there are no chances of them to escape, remember that these pets are no ordinary ones, they are highly intelligent and can often dig themselves a path out of such situations, as they do not like being restricted to a certain area.

You can build a pen and set the posts yourself; you have a clear idea of how much space you want the pen to occupy, so it will not take long, and will not cost much. Many owners prefer professionals to do the job as they are experts, and will take every precaution so that your potbelly or potbellies do not run away, but remember that this will cost you a bit extra.

Chapter 17: Activities

Besides making a mess of everything, potbellied pet pigs love and enjoy activities of all sorts. You must remember that in some states and countries, before you can take your pet pig on a walk, permission is needed in order to do so. The copy must be distributed to neighboring authorities as well.

Walking
Pigs love going on walks. They love to meet and make new friends as well, as they are very social. Pot bellied pigs are easy to take along on walks as well, which is a quality you can use to your advantage, especially if the pig is very energetic. All you have to do is attach a leash on yours and take it outside and let it blow off some steam with a nice, long walk.

Pools
In order to maintain their temperatures, and to give them a whole range of entertainment, let them swim in kiddie pools. Plastic pools are more preferable as they can easily chew and make holes.

Exploration
Let the potbellied wander around, but do not let them out of your sight. They love to discover new things and it is also very healthy for their brains as well. Let them go where they want to, but make sure there are no wild animals, especially dogs nearby. These two animals do not get along and must be kept separate.

Tricks & Treats
Your smart pets can learn many cool tricks, and they can be kept entertained from them as well. Teaching your pet potbelly simple tricks such as 'roll' or 'jump' can be very fun for the both of you.

Rooting

Since you already know how much your pet loves to root, let it out every now and then. It's a good thing if pigs are allowed to do what they are naturally good at. It helps them grow and mature too. Stopping them from indulging in their natural instincts will only result in one very frustrated potbelly.

Therapy with Other Animals

Pigs and dogs as you know are not on good terms. There are other animals that do not get really well with other pets at first. Over time though, they can be trained to get along. This can be a great way to socialize for your pet pig. The pig will get a chance to interact and open itself to many other kinds of animals, making healthy relationships. The pet will also get a certificate at the end of the course to certify it is a sociable pet.

Chapter 18: Toys & Accessories

Pigs love to run out in the wild, you have nothing to worry about at all. You can also give them toys but since they have very sharp teeth and very powerful jaws as well, not every toy will be suitable for them. Pig toys are much more durable, and they are stronger compared to other pet toys as well, and are even long lasting. There is a huge variety for you to take your pick from.

Types of Toys

If the pig is a piglet and a little under 8-12 weeks of age, it has not been separated from its mother for a long period of time. Till that age, pigs are used to having their mother's teats in their mouth to chew on, and as a source of food. Piglets will try to get other objects in their mouths at that point as well, which is why the most preferred toy for them at that certain age are balls, and paper bags too. Cat chew toys, dog chew toys, and even human infant toys can be given to the young piglet as well.

Toys which have parts and accessories such as clips and buttons should be kept far away from the potbelly. All toys also have to be pig-proof just like your entire household. The pet can easily choke on small things which come out of toys, specially a piglet.

Rooting Toys

This can be very hard to control; pigs love rooting, and there is nothing you can do to stop them. This is why you should let them carry out this natural feeling. You can purchase toys like a sandbox or rooting box to make sure your pet potbelly not only enjoys the natural process of rooting, but also does not root through your carpet or feet. If potbellies cannot be given space to root, they will mess up your entire carpet, and your feet will be in a lot of pain as well. As they grow older, their hooves will hurt you more, so it is better not to ignore this.

Obstacle Courses

If you want your pig to enjoy itself, make it an obstacle course. Do not add anything too difficult for it. Throw in a small rocking chair for your pig to enjoy. Add a slide to the pool so that your pet potbelly can make the best of it. You can be as creative as you want to be. There are certain precautions which are important before you start preparing the jungle gym. Make sure your pig cannot get any wounds, cuts, fractures and bruises. Also, make sure all screws, wood chips, and other tools are unreachable to the pet pig.

Rings and Floaters

If you want to, you can buy rings as well as floaters for your pet potbelly as well. Teach your potbellied pig how to swim and let them enjoy themselves in the pool all day long. In order to give it some company, throw in a couple of friends, such as rubber ducks, turtles, fishes, and other toys which are water proof; you can even throw in a couple of floating balls as well.

Chewing Toys

Give your pig doggie chew toys. You can easily find chew toys for dogs at any local shop and market. Use them as entertainment for your pet potbelly as well.

Stuffed Toys

Stuffed toys can only work in one condition, if your pig is trained, and you are sure it will not rip the toy apart. Stuffed toys are a bit dangerous around potbellies, as there is no telling what they will do to the toy unless they have been trained to behave. If so, let them snuggle into a bear, or duck, even a stuffed dog at night.

Petting

Petting may seem a lot of fun, but you should not make it into a habit. For potbellies, being petted is the best thing that could have and that can happen to them, but as they grow older, picking them up and placing them on your lap for naps will be a lot more difficult than it seems.

Tents & Camps

You can build your potbelly its very own campout site. Let the pig roam around, in and out, but be sure to use old sheets and rags for this play. They will tear them apart, rip them into shreds too if they are in a good mood.

Clothing

Many pet owners love to play dress up with their pet potbellies. The most suitable age for this is when the pig is 8-12 weeks old. You can dress it as a cowboy, a princess, which ever form you want to see them in. Give them a pair of boots, an adorable hat, take part in a fashion show, and even walk the ramp with them as well.

The piglets like getting a chance to play dress-up, it lets them interact with you as well as other animals and humans involved too.

Hide & Seek

If you have an old pair of sneakers, boots, or any kind of shoes and jeans, you can play hide and seek with your pet potbelly and transform the un-used item into a toy as well. Hide a nice treat inside and let your potbelly figure out a cunning way of how to get it. Time your potbelly on how fast it is and how long it takes it to get to the treat.

There are many types of accessories you will need to keep around the house for your potbelly.

Odor

Pig odor is very strong and definitely unwanted and unattractive. In order to stop the stench from spreading you will need something which absorbs the smell. Accessories and products such as OdorMute are very useful for this purpose. The natural enzymes in this product prevent the stink from traveling through the air to other parts of the house.

Thermometer

Your pig will get very uncomfortable and start squirming if it is stuck with a thermometer. This is why a normal one will not help you here; at the most, you will get ten seconds to get the result you need to properly check if the potbelly has a high temperature. Products such as the 9 seconds digital thermometer do exist, and are very easy to use. These thermometers are water and pig-proof as well.

Gloves

If your pig has flaky skin, you can use rubber gloves to gently get rid of the unwanted hair and flakes on its body hygienically. You can use the gloves to help give your pet a nice and proper bath as well.

Tablets

Many owners give their pets tablets to prevent them from being infected with dangerous infections and diseases. Have a talk with your pet's vet and purchase the medication and feed it to your pet according to the dose the vet has prescribed.

Ointments

These can be found online but it is better to ask a licensed and experienced veterinarian about these; they will prescribe ones that can suit your pet and heal it. Some will even purchase it on your behalf if you cannot find it at the local pet store.

Signs & Stickers

Show the world you love your precious potbelly by placing potbelly stickers in and around your house. Place them in the pet's room as wall decorators, and you can place the signs in front of your house as well.

Chapter 19: Pigs Comparison

Now, when you are purchasing a potbellied pig, there are other factors which you must take into consideration before purchasing it. You must remember as previously mentioned, adopting a pet pig is no joke, and is a tremendous responsibility as they are no ordinary pets.

You must be wondering why should you adopt a potbellied pig over other breeds of pigs and other animals as well, right? The answer is simple, compare the breeds and animals with each other, and you can see for yourselves why potbellies are preferred animals. Before we get on to the comparisons, you must first have an understanding of what domestic pigs are.

Domestic Pigs

Swines and Hogs are also known as domestic pigs. These pigs, hogs, and boars are those which are not exotic and wild, but they reside in farms. Domestic pigs are farmed as they are a source of pork and fat, but many in the United States and United Kingdom consider them not as livestock, but as pets.

The animal's hide, bones, and their bristles can be found being used in common products. If you see products with the word' 'gelatin' on them it probably has pig fat in the contents.

Potbellied Pigs VS Wild Hogs

Potbellied pigs and wild hogs belong to the same family, but are completely different. Wild hogs belong on the farm, whereas potbellies live in domestic environments like your home. Unlike wild hogs, potbellied pigs are trained to behave in the environment they receive. Wild hogs are next to impossible when it comes to training, as they will not listen to the owner, or trainer, no matter what their age may be.

They even have different eating habits and habitats as well. Wild hogs do like any sort of restrictions, whereas potbellied pigs can easily adjust to their environment. You have to be very cautious with wild hogs, whereas you do not need to be as cautious with potbellies.

	Potbellied Pigs	Wild Hogs
Habitat	Adaptable	Non Adaptable
Diet	Adaptable	Non Adaptable
Nature	Friendly	Often un-Friendly

Potbellied Pigs VS Farm Hogs

Farm hogs are raised by farmers for food. The farmers use the pork for their use, and often sell it, as well as other useable material to local markets for money. Farm hogs are reproduced so that this chain of supply can be continued throughout. On the other hand, potbellied pigs are considered as pets. They are not used for livestock purposes, and are not high maintenance.

Farm hogs need to be fed quite a lot, as the more they eat, the fatter they become, which is good for the farmer, whereas the potbellied pig does not need to consume such amounts of food. You can plan a schedule of when you want to feed the potbelly, according to your wish. The potbelly will be adjusted to that particular schedule as well.

nother thing you must know is that potbellies are not used for breeding purposes, some owners do not have space for piglets; you can breed them if you like to, and this depends on you completely. Since most owners do not do that, you do not have to spend money on vet visits during a pregnancy, you can save money on materials, and the male potbelly will not be aggressive and can be considered as a pet. As mentioned before, it gets hard to control the males once they can impregnate.

Potbellied Pigs VS Other Breeds

Potbellies are considered the best breeds to be cared for and adopted as domestic pets. This is due to several reasons, such as:

	Potbellied Pigs	**Other Breeds**
Costs	$1,000- $1,500 £641-£962 (per year)	$2,000-$3,000 £1,026-£1,920 (per year)
Habitat	Adaptable	Not always Adaptable
Health Care	$ 1,200 £770 (per year)	$2,500 £1,600 (per year)
Feed	$1,000 £641 (per year)	$2,500-$3,000 £1,600-£1,925 (per year)
Other Supplies	$500-$750 £320-£481	$1,000-$1,500 £641-£962
Behavior	Trainable	Not always Trainable
Expenses	$1,000-$1,500 £641-£962	$2,500-$3,000 £1,604-£1,925

Potbellies VS Dogs

As you know by now both animals, the dog and the potbellied pigs do not get along unless the animals have been through behavior therapy sessions. Aside from this fact, dogs are high maintenance, compared to pot bellied pigs.

Dogs have a different diet, they need to go on walks, have different activities, different living styles, and much more. They are similar to the potbellied pigs in many ways as well though; they can obey and understand their master, learn tricks, and learn to adapt in their surrounding environments as well. When it comes down to expenses, dogs are costlier to take care of compared to the potbellied pigs. This includes medical costs, toys and supplies, bedding supplies, expenses for making dog houses, etc.

Potbellies VS Cats

Unlike dogs and their aversion to potbellied pigs, cats tend to have a more positive bond with the pigs. Pigs and cats are somewhat alike in their natures as well, they are domestic pets which do not bother their masters much, both are seen roaming around in their own fantasy world, but, unlike pigs, cats are lazy. Pigs are active; they love to learn and perform many new tricks and are social animals too. Though cats are smaller in size, as well as weight, they lie around all day without giving entertainment, where as with potbellied pigs, each day is full of fun and adventure.

Did You Know?

Unlike cats, potbellied pigs love to swim and enjoy long hours in the cool water, and mud too.

Potbellies VS Other Animals

When you compare potbellied pigs to other animals, you can see that they are easier to handle, and afford. You may say that pets like parrots and fish are more affordable, as compared to the potbellied. That is true, but fish and parrots are not as talented as the potbellied pigs are. Here is a table to help explain this further.

	Potbellied Pigs	Fishes	Parrots
Tricks	Yes	No	Limited
Talk	No	No	Yes
Social	Yes	No	Yes
Understanding	Yes	No	Limited
Travel	Yes	No	Limited
Habitat	Adaptable	Restricted	Adaptable
Enjoyment	Yes	Limited	Limited

Chapter 20: Extraordinary Senses

Just like us humans, all pigs have 5 senses too. Some piglets which are born with complications and deficiencies may not, but potbellied pigs have one sense which not all animals have. Let us take a look at all of their six senses.

Sight & Hearing

Potbellies have very poor eyesight. All potbellies have this issue; their faces have folds and are smushed which makes it hard for them to see. This is from birth, since the moment a piglet potbelly is born, it has weak eyesight, which is why at times some piglets wander off away from their mother; all the more reason for you to be alert! They have a very keen sense of hearing; if you think you can sneak up on one, think again.

Smelling

Hide a treat such as a cookie in any part of the house, and your potbelly will find it within seconds. Yes, that is how sharp and keen their sense of smell is. Pigs are known for smelling truffles from below the ground too, which is why some restaurants use pigs to sniff them. They can even rip through any fabric and surfaces to get to the treat they smell, no matter how rough and solid it may be. You can say that in this matter they are very stubborn and will not rest until and unless they have that treat.

Tasting

You will laugh at this but, unlike other animals that do not really care what meal is in their bowls or on their plates, pigs actually do. As a matter of fact, they are like us humans, they will first go for an attempt towards bread, and then fish, followed by cheese, eggs, etc, and their last choice of options, just like ours, are vegetables. Isn't that really interesting and amazing at the same time?

Touching

Pigs just like pet dogs, love to be petted. Their skin tends to itch a lot, which is why if you rub or slightly scratch one, they will fall in love with you and will want lap petting every now and then. Do make sure of two things, one, do not use your bare hands while scratching your potbelly, wear gloves, and stay alert for any contact to your skin. Secondly, do not make lap petting a habit, as the potbelly grows older, it will be hard for you to fit it on your lap.

Pheromones

Pigs cannot read your mind, so you have nothing to worry about, but they can sense a lot, things like thoughts and emotions through pheromones. This is basically a sense pigs, and humans have which is related to our sense of smell. Let us say that your pig is in the backyard, and all of a sudden a wild dog appears. The dog will not attack the pig suddenly, it will monitor its prey, and will move towards it one step at a time, trying not to give its motives away. Luckily for the pig, the dog will give off pheromones, alerting the pig that someone wants to have it as dinner. The pig will run towards safety, or make noises such as snorting to alert the owner, that something is wrong.

Chapter 21: Ageing

Like humans and other animals, domestic and wild, pigs age. This is a normal process which can be seen in potbellied pigs around the age of 14. Since potbellied pigs have a life span of an average of 15-20 years, their approximate ageing also starts towards that age.

Effects of Ageing

Ageing can be dynamically spotted during the lifespan of a potbellied pig. You can take it to the vet, who can tell if its brain size is decreasing. This happens when the potbellied senior pigs are starting to become completely dependent on their owners.

Once the ageing process starts, the organs as well as physical and mental faculties of the potbellied pig start to degenerate. It will not remain active and digestion of food will also take longer and will be much harder. This is why you must consult with your vet of what to do and which changes to bring in the pet's diet.

More Symptoms

The potbellies start to lose their vision when they age. They will also turn deaf, senile, slow, and have very high chances of getting diseases such as arthritis. The senior potbellies will lose all interest in entertainment, competitions, and games too. They will require a warmer environment as their bodies cannot tolerate cold as they used to, and will be very picky when it comes to food.

Comfort is the one thing they will have all their attention towards, and until and unless they get the required level of it, they will complain about it to get your attention. Too much heat or too little will bother them; they need the perfect temperature. They don't like humidity and will stop eating. It will also develop wrinkles on its face and its body. These are all signs pointing towards the fact that a potbellied pig has entered the last stage of its life.

Chapter 22: Terminologies

It can get really confusing when many different terms are used to describe pigs, including potbellied pigs. Here is a list of common terminologies to help you out of this confusion. Listed below are the most common terms and their definitions. Keep in mind that these terms are very important, as several of them have been used throughout this entire book.

Terms

Barrow- Castrated Male Swine

Boar- Mature Male Swine

Feral Swine- A Male Boar

Farrow (Noun)- Litter of Piglets

Farrow (Verb)- Birth to Piglets

Hog- Domestic full-grown Swine

Pig- Immature Swine

Gilt- Unfertilized Female Pig (has never given birth)

Piglet- Very young Pig, a newborn Pig

Shoat- Weaned young Hog

Swine- A Hog

Sow- Female Matured Swine

Swineherd- Pig Farmer who attends to Swines

Queen- Unmated Female Pig

Chapter 23: How to Convince Your Parents

Often it is very hard to convince your parents, for almost everything and anything at all. What makes it harder to get their approval is the idea of having a potbellied pig or piglet running around in the house or its premises. If you really want the responsibility of a piglet which is none the less a human baby who needs love and care, and a mother, you must follow the following steps.

Step One: Maturity

The first thing which you must do is show your parents that you are mature enough to handle such a responsibility. Parents are the best and the only people who will give you the expert's advice on raising kids, if they say you are not ready, it means you are not.

In order to change their perception, you must show them you are in fact mature enough to be taking care of a baby pet on your own. Do not expect them to pitch in during the beginning; it will be you doing everything from feeding to cleaning.

Get up and out of bed on time, show your parents that you care about getting up early in the morning and can show maturity. Help your mother prepare breakfast, and help set up the table as well. This will give them a sense that you are responsible and will not let your potbellied pig starve.

Clean around the house, help in chores, and take care of tasks on time. Do remember that once you are in it, there is no coming out.

Step Two: Time and Utilization

You have to show your parents that having a pet will not mess around with your work, and studies either. Show this to them by covering all tasks on time, and complete all tasks on time as well. This will prove to your parents you are being responsible, and that you can easily manage all given tasks, as well as give time to your pet potbelly. If you leave the responsibility of your pet to your parents, they will not tolerate it for much longer.

Step Three: Take Initiative

Learn to take initiatives, if you have promised or if you have that you will complete a task, do complete it and do not leave it pending. This shows that you are lazy, which will eventually show to your parents you are not able to take the responsibility of a new member in the house.

Step Four: Motherhood

For males this term may seem a bit awkward, but taking care of a potbellied piglet is no less than taking care of a new born human child. You will have to feed it, clean up after it, train it, and you will have to be strict. Your parents will think you are not ready to handle such a responsibility as you know nothing about kids yet, show it to them.

Research online; ask friends and family members who own pets. Ask them about how tough it is to take care of pets, bring their pet home for a day or so and try to get the experience you are seeking. The best way to get this if a member in your family or a friend owns a potbellied pig, which is even better. Borrow the pet for a day and get a chance to interact with it up close and personally.

Ask your mother for advice, no one knows a child better than they do, you can ask dad as well, but they will in the end say ask mom. A mom is a mom no matter if she is a mother to a human or animal, all mothers have natural instincts.

Step Five: Use Their Cuteness

The biggest benefit you have on your side is the endless cuteness of potbellied pigs. Trick your mothers into sitting in front of the monitor with you use potbellied pig's pictures and show your mother how cute and adorable they are. Use the information you gained through this book and the Internet to tell your mother that you are now responsible, and ready to adopt a potbellied pig.

Convincing dad will not be a hard thing to do once mom says yes, which is why you must show your mom that you really are ready for the responsibility of the pet and you will not back away from it either.

Conclusion

Once you have successfully shown to both parents that you can be responsible, mature, and that you can accept the embrace of motherhood, it is time you got yourself a baby potbelly.

Chapter 24: Positives & Negatives

In this chapter, we will now summarize all the positives and negatives of owning a potbellied pig as a pet. All aspects have been taken into consideration and are mentioned below. Read through both sections very thoroughly.

Positives of Owning a Potbellied Pig

There are many reasons why owning a potbelly can prove to be positive. A potbelly pig is trainable once it is 8 weeks old which means you will not have to worry about training it from any aspect; this includes its behavior, potty, and diet as well.

Another positive factor of potbellies is that they are very social. They can easily interact with humans, especially children, and other pets as well. They will need to undergo behavior therapy to get along with dogs.

Potbellied pigs are affordable, you can restrict them to a specific diet, and they will follow it. They can also learn and perform tricks, and love to entertain. You can teach them many cool tricks, and let them perform in competitions, and take them in pet shows as well.

Potbellied males and females are easy to take care of as long as they are neutered and spayed. They enjoy almost every kind of activity and do not make a fuss about not sleeping in your room, with you, on your bed.

Negatives of Owning a Potbellied Pig

We got through the list of the positive aspects of owning one; now let us take a look at the negative ones. Owning a potbellied pig is not easy, and you definitely cannot take it lightly as a joke. Lots of time will be required in the care and nurturing of the potbelly pig. Since they are most preferable as piglets, they will need all of your time.

You will have to put them through the training process which is also very time consuming, and if you hire a professional to do it for you, it will cost you money. The same goes for training your potbelly to be social; it will take a lot of time, and if you hire someone else to do it for you, it will cost you.

Another negative thing about them is their natural aversion to dogs. Pigs are naturally preys to dogs, and other animals which hunt. To force them to get along will be a pain, and there is no telling what will happen if you leave both of them alone together.

Through genetics, potbellies can catch diseases, and infections as well. Other diseases will be expensive when it comes to treatment and the medication will only add to the bill. The pig may also have to be put down if the disease is severe. This means all the time you put towards the love and care, and all the money you had invested will all go to waste within minutes.

Unlike cats, dogs, and other pets, you need special permission to get a pet pig, to take it on walks, and you will have to neuter or spay it in order to prevent unwanted behavior.

Another negative reason why most people think twice before owning a potbelly is that they have to pig-proof every inch of the entire house, as well as the outside premises, and everywhere where it can go. This is because they love to put anything they find, and everything they find right in to their mouths. This is why the chances of them chocking is quite high.

Their temperatures always remain high, as they cannot sweat and keep cool. You will have to make sure your pig has access to water, or mud. You will also have to make sure the water is clean, and is changed every day.

Ointments, toys, harnesses, crates, etc, many accessories will be good for your potbelly. You will need the ointments to take care of its itchy or diseased skin or else it will whine about it to you, and make you very angry. Toys will be needed as pigs love to chew, and they need some source of entertainment. Crates are important as they are the only way your potbelly can be transported from one place to another with ease.

If the potbelly is living outside the house, precautions must be made for it to live in every kind of weather, and a pen or pig house must be made as well. If you make the house yourself, you will need to make sure every aspect has been properly covered and checked, and if you ask a professional to do it for you, this will cost you more.

Potbellies are naturally territorial. This includes their human, or their owner showing affection and concern towards another animal as well. Potbellies can naturally sense when another animal or pet is getting more affection.

A grownup potbellied pig is more difficult to train, and at times impossible. If it had not been trained as a piglet, it can defecate around the entire house, jump and break your furniture, as well as its own bones, and will rip through anything you give it. This is why you have to be extremely cautious and careful.

Chapter 25: 15 Pig-tastic Celebs who Own Potbellied Pigs

Owning potbellied pigs actually started to become a trend after some of the most famous celebrities started to make them as pets of their own. Here are the 15 celebrities who have taken the initiative in loving, taking care, and giving their own pet potbellied the world. Who knew celebs had a thing for this breed?

Megan Fox
Who does not recognize her? She is one of the most dominating actresses in Hollywood. She had a pet pig named Piggie Smalls. The model turned actress says the following. "Before we got our pig, I used to eat pork and now I can't. It's sad to think they are just slaughtered for hotdogs and breakfast meats. They aren't people, but they understand and they feel."

Paris Hilton
Another celeb who is known for owning potbellied pigs is the one and only, Paris Hilton. The heiress, fashion designer, television producer, film producer, entrepreneur spoils Princess Pigelette and gives her all the attention any pet would love.

Miley Cyrus
Just recently, in 2014, Miley Cyrus, adopted a baby potbelly named Bubba Sue. This adorable piglet became the young singer and actor's ultimate favorite pet.

George Clooney
Mr. Clooney had Max, the potbellied pig living with him for about 18 years. They were extremely attached and Max lived in Mr. Clooney's Mansion. Sadly, after living a full and fulfilled life, it passed away at age 20.

Elizabeth Hurley
This film producer and model/actress actually bred potbellied pigs in 2008. She became a professional and loves them with all of her heart.

David Beckham & Victoria Beckham
Who does not know about this Soccer Legend? Mr. and Mrs. Beckham have two adorable micro sized potbellied pigs which are just too cute; you cannot resist their cuteness, trust me. Both couples just adore their pets.

Denise Richards
Another famous television producer, model, and actress, Denise Richards is a firm advocate of owning potbellied pigs as pets. Her pet pigs were actually featured on her reality show as well called "Denise Richards: It's Complicated."

Tori Spelling
Tori and her family welcomed their new pet Hank into the family in 2011. Her children cannot get enough of Hank, take him on long walks and play with him all day long.

Danielle Steel
Danielle is a huge fan of dogs, and potbellied pigs too. All of her pet dogs and pigs go absolutely great together since all of them were made to go through special behavioral training.

Charlotte Church
Charlotte adopted two adorable potbellied pigs in the year 2008. She is an amazingly talented actress and singer, and has a thing for pet potbellies as well.

Rupert Grint
Famously recognized for his role in Harry Potter as Ron, Rupert Grint has two micro potbellied pigs named Stanley and Oscar. Recently, Oscar passed away. Rupert has other pets such as rats, turtles, dogs, and cats too.

Jonathan Ross
The comedian, screenwriter, and a man of many skills, Jonathan Ross has two cute little micro potbellies as pets.

Tom Daley
The man known for his skills in the pool, Tom Daley, is also known to be fond of potbellied pigs. In 2013, Daley had announced that he had adopted a pet potbellied named Robby-Ray.

Kendall Schmidt
The talented actor, singer, and dancer, Kendall Schmidt, known for his outstanding performance and comedy on Big Time Rush, has a pet potbellied named Yuma.

Trends
Since the world saw how enthusiastic these stars were towards the potbellied pigs, the trend of keeping it for aesthetic purposes caught on. Pigs were not famously known as being suitable as pets, until these celebrities showed it to the world.

Conclusion

Now that you have read, and understood how to care of a potbelly, how to train it, potty train it, and now that you have learnt all the negatives and positives about one, you can make your final decision, the important decision of owning a potbellied pig.

"I am fond of pigs. Dogs look up to us. Cats look down on us. Pigs treat us as equals."
— Winston S. Churchill

Make sure you know all of the instructions before you decide to purchase a potbelly. Firstly, you will have to learn about the laws of owning a potbellied pig in your state or country. Once you have done that, visit the breeder and ask every single question which comes to mind, and the ones mentioned previously in this guide. Buy a potbellied pig from a pure and professional breeder only.

Take it regularly to the vet for vaccines, pig-proof your entire house and surrounding areas as well. If you have other pets, talk to an expert behavior specialist regarding the behaviors of your pet. Train your pet strictly and maintain a regular diet.

If you wish to breed potbellied pigs yourself, mate the pigs, or else get your potbellied pet spayed and neutered. If the female potbelly is about to expect, make sure you have made all possible arrangements to ease delivery and do not forget to have your vet by your side as well.

If you wish to socialize your pig, take precautions and follow the instructions previously given.

Owning a potbellied pig is a huge responsibility, and not as different as taking care of a child. You can have a potbellied pig as a pet, but only if you are ready in every possible aspect. You are the mother and the father; you cannot lose your cool with the pet. You must feed it, bathe it, love it, care for it, travel with it, take it for regular checkups, and you must make sure that the potbellied pig is happy in every possible way it can be.

As you can see, potbellied pigs are the most suitable pets compared to other breeds of pigs. They are also considered as preferable pets as compared to other domestic pets, as they are more social, fun to play with, are trainable, and adapt to children, other pets, and to the environment without facing any particular problems.

Congratulations! You are finally ready to adopt your very own potbellied pig.

Good Luck!

References

There are many websites from which you can find the products you need for your new potbellied pig. The following is a list of references you can use and refer to while purchasing items and accessories for your pet.

Before you buy any product online, be sure to ask your vet for their advice. It is highly possible they can provide you with the materials you require; for the rest, you can take your pick from these.

Toys & Accessories

Here is a list of reference sites where you can buy toys and accessories for your pet potbellied pig, or piglet. You can even check the links for great ideas as well.

http://www.pigs4ever.com

http://www.backyardchickens.com

http://www.lushome.com

http://www.ebay.com or ebay.co.uk

http://www.schleich-s.com

You can even visit a local toy store and buy many toys from there as well. Just remember to buy those toys which will not be easy to choke on for your potbelly, and has no accessories or parts which come off easily.

Food & Water

You can ask a local pet store, or your potbellied pig's vet from where you can find its feed, you can even ask the store owner or vet to order it for you. Remember, keep it on a very strict diet, and change its diet when necessary, after consulting with a vet. Also, remember to give your potbellied pig access to water 24/7.

Fencing & Pens

You can build the fences and pen for you potbellied pig yourself. Make sure the fences and the posts are deep in the ground, are sturdy, and durable as well. Pigs will dig trough and find any way possible to get themselves out of the pen or cage.

You can always hire a professional as well, but it will cost extra.

Clothing & Accessories

Many pet owners love to dress their pets as if they were their own children. Many kids even enjoy playing dress-up with children, as you can recall, pigs are social and friendly, and so they do not mind being the center of attraction. You can buy their clothes or stitch them yourselves.

You can buy readymade clothes from any local store. They can easily fit in to the size and clothes of new born human babies. That should make it easy for you. If you want to find booths and booties, you can buy new born booties for them, and use boots from live sized dolls to fit the potbelly if you cannot find them elsewhere. Visiting a nearby toy shop is also a good idea as well.

Keep in mind that many clothing have buttons, and prints which can come off. Your potbelly has very sharp teeth and jaws. It is easy for the pet to stick the accessories within its mouth and choke on it. Make sure the boots and booties are pig-proof as well.

Published by IMB Publishing 2015